BE STRONG & COURAGEOUS

A Story of Love & War

Joe & Kathy Wasmond

Copyright © 2013 by Joe & Kathy Wasmond

Be Strong & Courageous
A story of love & war
by Joe & Kathy Wasmond

Printed in the United States of America

ISBN 9781626977952

All rights reserved solely by the author. The author guarantees all contents are original and do not infringe upon the legal rights of any other person or work. No part of this book may be reproduced in any form without the permission of the author. The views expressed in this book are not necessarily those of the publisher.

Unless otherwise indicated, Bible quotations are taken from the New American Standard Bible (NASB). Copyright © 1960, 1962, 1963, 1968, 1971, 1972, 1973, 1975, 1977, 1995 by The Lockman Foundation. Used by permission. All rights reserved.

Cover Design by Rob Eidemiller.
Printing Image, Knoxville, TN

www.xulonpress.com

Praise for
Be Strong & Courageous

"If you feel you have never experienced being in battle, you need to read ***Be Strong & Courageous: A story of love and war.*** Here you will be reminded that each of us is in a battle every day against this evil world. Joe & Kathy Wasmond do a great job of inter-weaving his very real Vietnam combat experiences as a Huey helicopter gunship pilot, battling it out with the Vietcong and North Vietnamese military forces in the Mekong Delta and their life as a couple. Put on your shield and stand guard 24/7 while you rely on God to see you through this daily battle of darkness. With Him in your fox hole, you can be relieved of a lot of that awful enemy pressure while Satan attempts to breach your perimeter."

William E. Peterson – Vietnam helicopter crew chief and door gunner (1967-68) U.S. Army Purple Heart Hall of Fame with three purple hearts
Author of ***Missions of Fire & Mercy & Chopper Warriors***

"The military spends years training our troops how to prepare for, fight and win our nation's battles. This book draws on that same mindset to instill an understanding that we can prepare for, and overcome our spiritual battles as well."

> Colonel Owen Ragland (Retired USAF) F-15 Fighter Plot

≈

"As Jesus often used stories to make His points, Joe & Kathy have done a great job of using vivid, real- life combat and life experiences to drive home the reality of spiritual warfare in today's world...and to provide critically important strategies for winning the battles we all face."

> Dr. Timothy Warner - Author of *Spiritual Warfare*, International Speaker & Professor of Missions

≈

"This book speaks, in real terms, about experiences of a combat helicopter pilot in Vietnam. As a veteran of that war, I can assure you many like me look at that conflict and the impact it has had on their lives…in ways the average American does not. Most importantly, the book sensitizes readers to the need to have a spiritual warfare battle plan for their own lives."

> Brigadier General Dick Abel (Retired USAF) Former Executive Director, Military Ministry, Campus Crusade for Christ

Praise for Be Strong & Courageous

"Not only does ***Be Strong & Courageous*** have balance and biblical foundations that will help any Christian deal with the spiritual battles of life, it has a message of healing insight that every soldier and war veteran will find compelling. Its message of hope is a much needed word for our time."

Dr. Mark Bubeck - Biblical Counselor and author of ***Overcoming the Adversary***

≈

"Thank you, Joe & Kathy, for sharing your new book. We have found memories of you as we ministered together in Kenya and at the JAARS Center in Waxhaw, N.C. May God bless this endeavor and encourage you as He continues to work through you to love on others as you have done in so many other countries around the world. How courageous you both are! A real illustration of God's undying love for all of us and the fulfillment of His plan in our lives (Jeremiah 29:11)."

Steve & Kathy Womack – Wycliffe Bible Translators

≈

"***Be Strong & Courageous*** is a must read book for all who long for a victorious Christian life. "

Dr. Benjamin Sawatsky
Former Executive Director, Evangelical Free Church, International Missions

"God often brings His message to the masses through His prophets. He has done that with Joe & Kathy. They bring their combat and life experiences from Vietnam and their marriage and balance that with Scripture to write this book for all of us. After reading **Be Strong & Courageous**, I was changed and my heart was set afire for God."

> Master Sergeant Jamie Harwick, USAF &
> President of the United Methodist Men, Desert Southwest Conference

≈

"A beautiful story of God's love, conquering life's, military, marital, cancer and spiritual battles. Great teaching tools for victory."

> Dr. Michael J. Wind
> Optometrist – Manitowoc, Wisconsin

≈

"***Be Strong & Courageous: A story of love and war*** by Joe & Kathy Wamond offers insight into God's undying love, whose patience is evident even in the darkest hours of wartime. It reminds us we are not alone in this world combatting the many forces that threaten our daily walk with the Lord. A powerful message of faith, determination and ultimately, love."

> Mrs. Mikey Hoeven
> Former First Lady of North Dakota

Praise for Be Strong & Courageous

"As Joe & Kathy so eloquently convey in ***Be Strong and Courageous***, adversity in our lives may be overcome through a daily commitment to aid one's fellow man…while at the same time expressing the necessity of maintaining individual integrity and principled courage. Their book provides, through the lens of military, personal and spiritual conflict an authoritative guide that serves as a moral compass to navigate the often difficult passages of life."

    Major General Terry "Max" Haston
    The Adjutant General of Tennessee

≈

"This book by Joe & Kathy Wasmond is truly an intelligence report to bring each person to victory. They help us understand the enemy's tactics. They remind us of our identity and the authority we have in our arsenals. No wise warrior goes into combat unprepared. Stop running from the enemy spiritually, know who you are in Christ and we will have victory. Then you will find peace."

    Major David R. Schlichter, U.S. Army
    Chaplain – First Cavalry Division. Call sign–
    Stallion Cross

≈

"I trained for the war in Vietnam. Joe trained, went, fought most honorably, survived, and returned home to tell about it. Kathy battled cancer, survived and lives to tell about it. Their battle in physical realms are analogous to spiritual warfare. They know it well and want to equip you for your battles you cannot avoid. Having loved and enjoyed Joe and Kathy Wasmond for over 25 years, Lois and I highly recommend *Be Strong & Courageous.*"

    Dr. Jim Anderson, Pastoral Care with the
    Evangelical Free Church
    Author of *For God's Sake, REST*

Table of Contents

Acknowledgments xi

1. A Love Story 13
2. We Were Soldiers Once...And Young 18
3. The Terror That Comes by Night 32
4. The Boy Becomes a Warrior 52
5. Armed and Dangerous 64
6. The Unseen Hand 74
7. Under Cover 86
8. Dirty Tricks 101
9. Prisoners of War 115
10. Friendly Fire 129
11. The Wall 146
12. Welcome Home Soldier 155
13. A Wife's Perspective of War & Marriage 168

Epilogue 173

Acknowledgments

No one in their right mind would choose to go to war. But when I was called upon in 1968 to fight for others in Southeast Asia so that they could enjoy the freedoms you and I many times take for granted, I willingly volunteered.

I want to thank my parents for instilling in me the values that have served me so well over my lifetime that helped me understand what it means to make a commitment to service and a righteous cause.

To my dear wife, Kathy, and our two precious daughters, Jennifer and Sarah: You married and were parented by a young man who saw and experienced the horrors of war that no one should have to deal with. You three women, more than anyone else in my life, have endured the consequences of my time in Vietnam. Your unconditional love and acceptance along with your undying encouragement is still bringing me through my wartime experiences. You have all added immeasurably to my life and this book. It is as much your story as it is mine.

Finally, this book is my tribute to the brave soldiers I fought alongside with in Vietnam from 1969 to 1970 as a combat helicopter pilot. I watched as some of them died on the battlefields doing my best to protect and rescue them. I can still see the blood of the dead and wounded spilled on the floor of my helicopter cargo bay as we extracted them from hot LZ's. This memory would also be true of any soldier who has served in military combat in whatever arena of battle they fought.

For the brave Vietcong and North Vietnamese soldiers who died by our hands, I want to acknowledge them as formidable adversaries. They too were sons, husbands and fathers.

To every man or woman who has ever put on a military uniform in the service of your country, I salute you. As Lt. General Hal Moore and Joseph Galloway stated so well in the prologue to their book, "This is your story and theirs. For we were soldiers once…and young" (p. xxv).

Thanks & appreciation to Mary Brown, our youngest daughter's mother-in-law, for her editing and corrections; Rob Eidemiller for the cover design, and Sabrina Dowdy for some of the photos.

And never forget God's charge to Joshua over three thousand years ago and to us today:

> *"Be strong and courageous, for you shall give this people possession of the land which I swore to their fathers to give them. <u>Only be strong and very courageous;</u> be careful to do according to all the law which Moses My servant commanded you; do not turn from it to the right or to the left, so that you may have success wherever you go" (Joshua 1:6-7).*

Chapter 1

A Love Story

I came home from a ministry trip to Nigeria in August of 2008. Kathy wasn't feeling well and was diagnosed with Stage Four Mantle Cell Lymphoma, a rare form of blood cancer. Since then we have been on a much different journey than when we first met in 1965 and all of the ministry trips we have done together in 65 countries over the last 30+ years.

I have a hand written note (see below) that Kathy gave me while she was going through her chemo therapy and then an autologous stem cell transplant. She wrote it from her hospital bed and gave it to me for Valentine's Day, 2009 after her third round of chemo therapy here in Knoxville, TN where we have lived since 1996.

It was necessary to have a double port inserted into the left side of her chest where the most advanced treatment ever developed for her type of cancer dripped through her veins for four days every month in the hospital for six months until she went into remission. We then moved to the Vanderbilt Cancer Clinic in Nashville,

TN for 45 days to do an autologous stem cell transplant from her own stem cells. They then surgically implanted another port called a Hickman Line on the right side of her chest with three tubes hanging out in order to infuse her own cancer fee cells back into her body after another round of chemo therapy. The following is what Kathy wrote.

*Once Upon a Time...*there were two teenagers who fell in love. She was 13 and he was 14. They spotted each other in their High School hallway long ago in a suburb of Chicago in 1965. He had blue eyes, blond hair and a dazzling smile. His eyes were filled with mischief. Anyone could see that this boy spelled trouble with a capital T. Nevertheless he was so handsome. She had beautiful, long auburn hair that he thought was so beautiful. He fell in love with her the minute he saw her. She had a sweet smile and every bit an honors student in her neatly pressed school uniform. They couldn't have been more different. He was a rebel and she was a princess.

After graduation from High School, he had to go fight a war in a faraway place called Vietnam as a helicopter pilot. She went on to become a nurse at a large hospital in the inner city of Chicago.

Each and every day she waited and prayed for his return, even though he wondered if she still cared for him. But when he came home from the war in 1970 they married at the age of 20 and moved into a 12' x 60' trailer outside Ft. Rucker, Alabama where he served as an instructor pilot.

They honeymooned in Panama City, Florida. It was a magical time of laughter and passionate love. He would always give her yellow roses and note cards at every anniversary telling her, *"I love you peanut"*. They danced and sang together in their little tin can of a house in the hot Alabama sun outside the Army base. They were very happy.

Over the years they grew more deeply in love. The picture books are filled with memories of their journey together.

Two years later they held their first born daughter in their arms where they were then living in Omaha, Nebraska after his military service. He helped her in the delivery room. He was also by her side when their second daughter was born in northern Wisconsin seven years later. He delivered their second daughter at home because the snow storm was too intense to leave their little house in the North Woods to get to the hospital 30 miles away that very cold wintery March night.

Then in their early thirties after giving their lives to Jesus Christ six years earlier they sold their house on the lake in Wisconsin and packed up all their belongings into barrels and crates shipping them to the rain forest of Central Africa that took one year to get there. They left their beautiful North Woods's home with their two daughters to begin their life long service as missionaries.

Once they arrived in Africa, they had to learn the language of the people they were sent to serve and immediately fell in love with their new African friends. They would host and honor them in their "modified mud hut" in this beautiful rain forest setting with no running water or electricity. Again, God provided everything they needed.

Then in their 40's and 50's God took them to 65 other countries, hand-in-hand to love on many other cultures and people groups. The cost was high, but the blessings cannot be measured.

Now as they approach their sixties, their hair has come and gone, and this 13 year old girl is surviving her battle with cancer. However, they are still enclosed in each other's arms. He shaved her head as she went through chemo therapy, but he told her, ***"I love you and you are so beautiful with or without hair."*** So, he shaved his head as well. They danced and sang together again just like those days in that trailer in Alabama.

Today as you look into their eyes you can still see the fire that was kindled when they were teenagers and spotted each other in a High School hallway long ago. They are still sweethearts and have come to understand what it means as they walk through life;

That for better or whatever they are in it together FOREVER.

Kathy to My Joe
Valentine's Day, 2009

P.S. On our 42nd wedding anniversary Kathy gave me a card that read:

If I wrote a Fairy Tale about us, it'd be just like an amazing dream, the most romantic love story ever told. And when I wrote the ending it would simply say…and they loved happily ever after.

"Let's make every day our happily ever after no matter what the circumstances. Thank you for being my wonderful husband."

I Love U,

Me

Chapter 2

We Were Soldiers Once... And Young

It was two days after Christmas, 1969 just five days after my 20th birthday. The night was very black as we patrolled the skies over the jungles and rice paddies northwest of Saigon, South Viet Nam (now called Ho Chi Minh City). All was quiet as I turned our nighthawk helicopter gunship around and headed back to our base camp at Cu Chi to refuel.

Cu Chi was a small farming community 18 miles from the Cambodian border. The enormous U.S. Army base camp built there during the Vietnam conflict was our home. Cleared by bulldozers and other heavy equipment, it was established by troops who slashed their way through thick jungle vegetation and enemy emplacements in order to provide a safe base of operations. There were over 20,000 of us living there and the airstrip could land any size aircraft. We had more take offs and landings than most U.S. airports do today.

Cu Chi became headquarters for the 2nd Brigade of the 25th Infantry's Tropic Lightning Division and many other units. It was one of the largest U.S. Army bases in Vietnam. It stood strategically between the North Vietnamese/Viet Cong strongholds to the north and Saigon to the south, thus making it also one of the most dangerous installations during the war. Saigon was, at the time, capital of South Vietnam, and the enemy's prime objective. As U.S. soldiers we were called to work with the local population to help them fight for and build their own democratic lifestyle and government, seeking to engage the enemy in the heart of Viet Cong controlled territory.

I was assigned to Company A of the 25th Aviation Battalion. Company B was known as the "Diamond Heads." They were an attack support or gunship helicopter unit, so we called them "Stingers." Company C flew Command and Control. We all flew any mission necessary for the support of our ground forces and filled a vital role in providing them with air mobility. Together, all three companies logged nearly 4000 flying hours per month. Our motto was, "We fly for the troops."

Our unit's call sign was the "Little Bears," named after a honey/sun bear captured and given to us by a Special Forces unit that our aviation company, before my arrival in country, had extracted from a hot landing zone (LZ) some years earlier. The image of this sun bear standing upright, clutching a lightning bolt, was stenciled on the noses and side panels of our helicopters as our unit's insignia.

They are called sun bears because of the bright orange diamond on their chests. We housed her in a cage in the middle of our compound. She was our personal pet and mascot. Every so often when she went into heat and escape her cage she would come running through our hootches looking for a mate. We all had some fun trying to catch and get her back into her cage. My personal call sign was "Little Bear 21" which I received in 1969 at age 19 after becoming an aircraft commander just a few months into my tour of duty.

Our mission that night was to provide gunship cover to protect the troops on the ground, including the numerous six-man ambush patrols scattered across the landscape below us. From our vantage point they appeared dug in and secure for the night.

Suddenly we saw tracer rounds from our own M-16's and enemy AK 47 rifles spewing in all directions. An ambush patrol, one of the units from the Second Battalion of the 14th Infantry was under serious attack. As we tuned in the battalion's radio frequency, the patrol leader was already calling for help. We could hear the sounds of close combat in our headsets as he keyed in his microphone. A much larger force had engaged them and their position was now being overrun by Viet Cong (VC) soldiers. We abandoned our refueling mission, banked hard 180 degrees and entered the battle zone below.

As soon as we arrived, we ejected flares over their position enabling all of us to see the attacking forces on the ground. We dove down from 3000 feet in a high overhead circling descent under our flares firing our mini-gun around the perimeter of our troop location. This weapon could deliver 4-6000 rounds per minute, and our gunner had to be careful not to hit our own men. All he had to guide him was a strobe light flashing from the helmet of one of our soldiers on the ground that we could see vertically, but could not be seen horizontally giving away their position. I was focused on maneuvering our helicopter in this accelerated descent to get into the landing zone (LZ) and get our troops out of there.

As we neared the LZ under the illumination of the flares, we observed enemy soldiers running freely through our intended touch down point. Turning on our landing lights at the last minute, the VC soldiers turned their fire upon us so intensely that we had to pull out.

By this time two of our soldiers were already dead and several more severely wounded. Other gunship helicopters were coming on site, but we needed help to extract our men. We radioed for more air and artillery support. F-4 Phantom jets scrambled out of Tan Son Nhut airbase in Saigon arrived overhead, ready to drop napalm on both sides of the LZ, while our heavy artillery fire pounded the perimeter around our troops.

We coordinated our second approach with the Phantoms and raced into the LZ just behind their bombing runs. I quickly dropped our helicopter toward the ground. As we landed, the heat from the napalm fire whooshed through our open cargo bays. What was left of this six-man patrol came running toward my aircraft, carrying the dead and wounded bodies of their comrades. They were followed by VC soldiers firing at us. Their bullets and mortars were exploding within yards of our helicopter. We shut off our landing lights and depended on the flares descending overhead to get our bearings.

I pulled out my own weapon and began firing out the window from the side door of the cockpit. I had no expectations of leaving that LZ alive, but we were not going to take-off without trying our best to get our men out of this hostile situation… even if it meant dying with them right there.

As our soldiers struggled to board the chopper, I noticed one of the soldiers was missing a portion of his leg, a tourniquet tied around his thigh to stop the bleeding. He was hoisted into our cargo bay. Heroically, one of his squad members rushed back into the LZ, retrieved his leg with the boot still attached, and jumped into the helicopter firing his M-16 with his free hand. The risk he took was not foolish. Our doctors and nurses back at the base camp field hospital had become miracle workers in repairing severed body parts and so chances were good this man's leg could be saved. It was well worth the wait in this hot LZ.

Dumping the remainder of our flares and ammunition in order to lighten our weight for take-off, we got out of there as fast as we could. Our skids bounced off the ground several times and we dragged through the grass before getting airborne. Seconds later we gained altitude and were soon wrapped in the safety of the dark skies, out of the reach of enemy fire below.

One month later I was awarded the Distinguished Flying Cross (DFC) for this action. I wasn't thinking of medals that dangerous night nor on any other mission I flew for that matter. My only concern was for my fellow soldiers that I was called and equipped to support. We were all just operating as a team taking care of one another.

The commendation they awarded me read as follows:

> ***"Receiving word that several friendly casualties had been sustained, Warrant Officer Wasmond fearlessly landed in***

a hostile area. With complete disregard for his own safety, Warrant Officer Wasmond exposed himself to the hail of fire as he remained in the perilous area until all the wounded were aboard his aircraft. His valorous actions contributed immeasurably to the success of the mission. Warrant Officer Wasmond's bravery and devotion to duty are in keeping with the highest tradition of military service and reflect great credit upon himself, his unit, the 25th Infantry Division, and the United States Army. By direction of the President, under the provision of the Congress of the United States."

Six months later, on June 6, 1970, I was awarded a second DFC for rescuing a downed helicopter crew involved in a night time resupply mission that had been shot down. Though the ground element notified me that there was not ample room for a safe landing, I carefully hovered down through the trees in the middle of the night and landed anyway. It never occurred to me not to rescue our fellow soldiers, even though the enemy fire was intense. Again I was just doing what they would have done for me.

I never knew who wrote those DFC citations. As I read them today over 40 years later in the safety and quiet of my home. I find it hard to remember that I acted as cited. All I know is that it never occurred to me not to come to the aid of a fellow soldier.

In retrospect, I now know that God was preparing me even before I knew Him, to bring Him glory by rescuing captive and wounded souls. It has become my mission in life to establish people free and complete in Christ so they can joyfully obey the Great Commandment (to love God and people) in order to fulfill their role in accomplishing the Great Commission (making disciples of all nations).

Writing this book has not been easy. I have had to face a lot of painful memories that I would much rather have ignored or forgotten. I put them in compartments of my mind, but they come back out from time to time when I least expect it, especially at night.

I have been asked a number of times. "When did you get home from the war?" I usually respond, "Last Night."

But this has also has been a healing time for me. I have fought hard not to let my past dictate my future, but have not always succeeded. No one who has ever been in combat will forget the sights, sounds and smells of war and the valiant enemy soldiers we killed. They too were sons, husbands and fathers. WAR SUCKS. That's Greek for "war sucks."

If you were one of those stationed in Southeast Asia between 1959 and 1975, or if you were deployed in any other war in the Middle East or any other country since, I pray that this book will be part of your healing journey as well. It's your story as much as it is mine.

If you have been graciously spared the experience of military combat, my prayer is that the Lord will enable you to translate my wartime and our marriage experiences into your present day reality so that you can understand that we are all engaged in the fight of our lives. It is a spiritual battle where we, as children of God, are called to take His truth in love to a world of increasing, encroaching darkness. As much as we might not want to face it, the truth is that every one of us lives each day of our lives on a cosmic battlefield called planet earth.

John Eldredge, in his book *Waking the Dead*, reminds us of the imagery of warfare against evil that fills our culture and literature:

> *"Little Red Riding Hood is attacked by a wolf. Dorothy must face and bring down the Wicked Witch of the West. Qui-Gon Jinn and Obi-Wan Kenobi go hand to hand against Darth Maul. To release the captives of the Matrix, Neo battles the powerful 'agents.' Frodo is hunted by the Black Riders. The Morgul blade that the Black Riders pierced Frodo with in the battle on Weathertop – it was aimed at his heart. Beowulf kills the monster Grendel, and then he has to battle Grendel's mother. Saint George slays the dragon. The children who stumbled into Narnia are called upon by Aslan to battle the White Witch and her armies so that Narnia might be free. Every story has a villain because yours does. You were born into a world at war." (p. 151)*

Kathy and I felt strongly that we should write a short primer about spiritual warfare, designed for both men and women. It is still our deep desire that this book will open up your eyes, ears and hearts to the reality of spiritual conflict that seeks to steal, kill and destroy lives, marriages, families, churches and even nations. We pray that you will be better equipped and more motivated to take your place of leadership and engage the enemy effectively in battle as a result of what we have written in this book.

We have also waged spiritual battle shoulder to shoulder with brave, godly women especially our wives and daughters. Kathy and our two daughters, Jennifer and Sarah, have all made significant contributions to and given valuable input into this book.

We conclude this book with the final chapter from my dear wife, Kathy, who provides her perspective on a journey that has inextricably involved her in spiritual warfare. She has also written some powerful parts in the other chapters. She has been my friend, wife, mother of our two daughters and ministry partner for our entire lives together.

As we begin this book on love and spiritual warfare, we feel it is wise to launch a preemptive strike against one of the more common maladies associated with the study of this subject: either attributing all our problems to the demonic or pretending that there is no spiritual battle going on and sticking our heads in the sand. C.S. Lewis, in the preface to his classic work, **The Screwtape Letters,** puts it this way:

> *"There are two equal and opposite errors into which our race can fall about the devils. One is to disbelieve in their existence. The other is to believe, and to feel an excessive and unhealthy interest in them. They themselves are*

equally pleased by both errors and hail a materialist or a magician with the same delight" (p.17).

Chances are slim that you are a disbeliever in the spiritual world or you would have likely tossed this book aside by now. The second temptation that Lewis warns against is much more subtle, however, therefore presenting a real and present danger.

When one begins to understand the reality of the spirit realm and our authority in Christ, it is so liberating that one can overdose on it all. An overly zealous believer can end up rebuking demons where there are none and foolishly charging into battles he or she is neither called nor equipped to fight. The pendulum swings to extremes more easily than you might imagine. It is true that Scripture warns us to, *"Be of sober spirit, be on the alert. Your adversary, the devil, prowls around like a roaring lion, seeking someone to devour"* (1 Peter 5:8). But we are to fix our eyes on Jesus, the author and perfecter of our faith (Hebrews 12:2), not on Satan. We are to "keep seeking the things above, where Christ is, seated at the right hand of God" (Col. 3:1), not on the things of earth where demons are.

If you are a child of God, you have already been seated in the heavenly realm, far above evil principalities and dark powers (Ephesians 2:6). The only way that Satan and his forces can take advantage of you is if you believe his lies and accusations or give into his temptations to sin.

When Jesus finished His all-night prayer vigil on the mountain and then summoned those He had chosen as apostles, His reasons for choosing them provide a healthy framework for all of us in keeping our spiritual priorities in order:

> *"And He appointed twelve, so that they would be with Him and that He could send them out to preach, and to have authority to cast out the demons."* (Mark 3:14-15)

Jesus' first priority for the twelve and for us is *to be with Him,* in an intimate, growing relationship with Him. This must always be at the top of the priority list for any believer in Christ to be spiritually healthy and balanced. You can't love Jesus too much! But it is dangerously easy to allow other things – especially ministry and even spiritual warfare – to become our first love.

The apostle John relayed a message from the Lord Jesus Himself to the church at Ephesus (Revelation 2:1-7). Ephesus was a hotbed for spiritual warfare in the first century due mainly to the city's rabid devotion to the pagan goddess Artemis, whose temple, one of the seven wonders of the ancient world, was located just outside the city.

Jesus' letter to the Ephesian believers commended them for their hard work and endurance in trial and even their intolerance of evil men and false apostles (Revelation 2:1-3). Quite a résumé! But what they had missed in all their *labor* for Jesus was a *love* for Jesus, and Jesus threatened to shut the whole operation down if they didn't get that one thing right (Revelation 2:4-5).

That's why Jesus' first purpose for calling the twelve was to be with Him in relationship and then secondarily that He could send them out to preach. Ministry is important, vitally important. Ephesians 2:10 even says that we are "God's workmanship, created in Christ Jesus for good works, which God prepared beforehand so that we would walk in them." God made us for good works! But our responsibility is to walk with Jesus who will lead us into the good works that He has already prepared for us to do. If we're not walking with Jesus, we'll end up doing our own thing and not His. God's good works for us always flow from an abiding relationship with Christ (John 15:1-8).

Finally, as we are walking with Jesus and preaching the good news, we will encounter the powers of darkness, and those held captive by them. Count on it. And so the Lord Jesus bestowed on the apostles and on us authority to cast out the demons. We'll talk later about a methodology of how to do that effectively, but for now suffice it to say that dealing with the demonic is never to be our primary or even secondary focus.

So why write this book? Good question. It is because the Apostle Paul's assertion that "we are not ignorant of his [Satan's] schemes" cannot honestly be made by a large portion of the Church in the West. Too many of us *are* ignorant of the devil's schemes and therefore he is able to take advantage of us (2 Corinthians 2:11). What starts out as an enemy **foothold** today can one day become a **stronghold**, and eventually even a **stranglehold** of control in one's life.

Clinton Arnold, in his excellent book ***Three Crucial Questions about Spiritual Warfare*** comments on the inevitability of war in the spiritual realm when he said:

> ***"Some believers are too frightened even to talk about spiritual warfare and thus try earnestly to avoid the topic***

> *altogether. Avoiding the topic is a profoundly inadequate response. Spiritual warfare is not an isolatable compartment of church ministry or Christian experience. Spiritual warfare is an integral part of the entire Christian experience. It is a fact of life. To think that a Christian could avoid spiritual warfare is like imagining that a gardener could avoid dealing with weeds. Our goal should be to gain an accurate and sober-minded understanding of spiritual warfare – not a view tainted by frightening superstitions and odd practices." (p.19).*

Arnold is right. Ignoring something doesn't make it go away, and avoiding spiritual warfare will become increasingly difficult in these last days before the return of the King. Jesus prophesied that things will get even more intense as false christs and false prophets will arise and will show great signs and wonders, so as to mislead, if possible, even the elect. "Behold, I have told you in advance." (Matthew 24:24-25).

Our desire and prayer is that this book will provide you with a motivational and practical battle plan for spiritual warfare with these analogies from actual combat experiences in Vietnam and our lives.

War is coming. It is, in fact, already here. The war started ages ago in a beautiful garden called Eden (Genesis 3), and will not be over until Jesus comes a second time to make all things new. There are only four chapters in the Bible that don't talk about warfare; Genesis 1&2 and Revelation 21 & 22. Are you prepared for battle?

Chapter Three

The Terror That Comes by Night

Nine years old is an awfully young age to go to war, but it was then that I first experienced the reality of the supernatural. It was 1959 and I was being raised in a great Catholic home, school and church environment that taught me many important truths about God. I was an altar boy for years but I was also taught that if I wasn't a good boy the devil would come during the night to "get me." That fear tactic failed to accomplish its purpose as I was usually in more than my share of trouble and I didn't fall for the scare tactic until one night!

I am the first born of 11 children. This particular year our family was living in a house without enough bedrooms for all of us. At that time I had four younger sisters who slept in the upstairs bedrooms while I slept in an attic area above the kitchen. It was a dark, unfinished space that could have frightened any young child.

My parents had just put us to bed and turned out the lights. I was trying to sleep, buried completely under my covers when I soon felt an evil presence in the room. I dared to peek out from under the bedspread, and there in the corner of the attic was a dark shadow. I froze with terror as I sensed it wanted to harm me.

After what seemed like hours, I mustered up enough courage to run from my attic bedroom downstairs to the first floor bedroom where my parents were sleeping. I hid myself under the dining room table in front of their bedroom door. I wanted so much to open their door and jump into bed with them, but I was afraid they would find my fear unfounded and foolish. After all, I was their oldest son and at nine years of age needed to be beyond such childish night terror experiences.

So I sat under the dining room table until dawn many nights without my parents knowing I was there. This went on for months until we finally moved from that house into a larger one with sufficient space to house six more brothers and sisters yet to be born.

Fast forward to 1974. Kathy and I had been married for four years (1970) after serving four years in the Army and one year in Vietnam as helicopter pilot (1969-1970). I then started a construction/remodeling business in a suburb of Chicago where we both grew up together. Our first daughter was two years old and life seemed to be on the upswing.

A new movie, **The Exorcist**, had just come out in theaters and foolishly I went to see it. For the first time, in cinema graphic detail, I saw my childhood terrors portrayed on a movie screen. I was traumatized by what I saw, but could not share my fears with Kathy. For years I had been having nightmares from my experiences in Vietnam that caused me to wake up many nights screaming and running for a bunker because of incoming mortar and rocket fire, but this night I would awaken for another reason.

I was restless much of the night and around 3:00am I became aware of an evil presence in our bedroom. It looked and felt like the same evil presence I experienced when I was nine years old. I was so startled by what I saw that I cried out with fear, waking up Kathy. I lied, telling her that it was just another nightmare from the war but I was shaken to the core knowing the evil presence from my childhood had returned to haunt me.

Later we moved to Eagle River, Wisconsin. Prior to that move both Kathy and I had received the Lord in a Baptist church in Elgin, Illinois in 1977. We were eager new believers looking for a new a start in life, a new home and a church. Though we found our little house in the north woods of Wisconsin on a beautiful lake, we spent two years finding the right church for us. We eventually became members of the Evangelical Free Church in Conover, Wisconsin.

On our second visit to this church, I sensed that same evil presence that I had experienced from my past. I was outraged and confused. I had believed that as a Christian I would never again have to encounter such spiritual trauma.

When I asked the pastor, who was a 20-year missionary veteran from Zaire, Africa, he explained that he and the elders had been ministering to one of the church member who had been involved in the occult. They were trying to deliver this professing believer from the demonic influences in her life. He also suggested that I might have the gift of discerning spirits.

I had no clue what he meant and didn't want anything to do with it!

During this same time period, our first daughter began waking up many nights with what we can only describe as bizarre night terror experiences. She was convinced there was something very frightening in her room and she could not sleep. We always turned on the lights looking under the bed and in the closet and spent many sleepless nights trying to comfort her without much success. To say that we were discouraged would have been an understatement and were forced to watch our precious first born go through the same night terrors I went through as a child and as an adult. We had no biblical instruction in how to handle this. Sadly, most Christians in America are in the same boat.

Our oldest daughter, now married with our first granddaughter, Jennifer (Wasmond) Levesque recalls her night terror experiences growing up:

"I was 9 years old when I accepted Christ as my Lord and Savior. My Dad held my hand that night as I prayed that life changing prayer. Shortly afterwards I began experiencing the same "night terrors" my father had experienced. Little to my knowledge at the time, God had already armed me with two very powerful weapons of warfare. The first weapon was that in becoming a child of God I entered into and came under God's protection and the second was my earthly father who was already a war hero and would also become mine.

The enemy targeted me in the form of a day dream. It was not just a "scary" day dream of a witch holding me as a prisoner in shackles but it was a real and terrifying presence that I sensed. That day dream soon became a nightmare. I remember recalling the specifics of that nightmare to my parents after I had woken them up one night terrified and feeling as if something was suffocating me. We prayed together authoritatively in Jesus name and I went back to feeling safe and sound.

I would encounter the same demonic enemy several years later in Barrington, Illinois when one afternoon as I was walking up a flight of stairs from our family room. I sensed something behind me. It was almost right on top of me wanting to specifically get over me, envelope me and choke me. When I finally got to the top of the stairs, I fell to the floor barely able to breathe. This was not just the same feeling you have from watching a scary movie or being afraid of the dark. This was a real and somewhat powerful entity that I did not unserstand.

I was living in Miami with my family where my parents were planting a bi-lingual church and I had just started college when the enemy once again attacked. I was sleeping deeply one night and I remember it being such a restful sleep and suddenly out of nowhere I could not breathe and I was being choked by something invisible. The feeling was so supernatural and overpowering that I had to make sure it was really happening and that I was not just having a horrible nightmare so I made myself open my eyes and attempt to sit up. I could only open my eyes as my body was pinned down by an unseen force. I was utterly terrified. I cried out the word Dad several times but I was being choked so badly that the word Dad was hardly audible. I remember tears streaming down my face and being soaked in sweat from fighting to sit up. But a power came over me just as I thought I would not be able to even attempt to yell out for help again. I sat up and screamed out one word. Jesus! All I remember is the silence and that I was safe and being held by my earthly father and hero who heard my cries for help."

What was going on? Were my daughter and I simply victims of an overactive imagination? Were we seeing a ghost, the spirit of some poor, departed soul? Were we the victims of a psychotic episode or some other mental illness?

David Hufford in researching night terror experiences in several different cultures and through the literature of the last several hundred years, would have categorized my childhood experience as "being hagged." He states the following in his book, *The Terror that Comes by Night: An experience-centered study of supernatural assault traditions (p.10-11):*

"The term is derived from Newfoundland folklore about the Old Hag and Nightmare. The term 'nightmare' literally means 'night demon,' formerly referring to an evil spirit that was believed to haunt and suffocate sleeping people." Hufford summarizes the folklore tradition in the following four possible elements:

1) Awakening (or an experience immediately preceding sleep);
2) Hearing and/or seeing something come into the room and approach the bed;

3) Being pressed on the chest or strangled;
4) Inability to move or cry out until either being brought out of the state by someone else or breaking through the feeling of paralysis on one's own. This experience is explained as caused by either a supernatural assault, indigestion, circulatory stagnation, or some combination of them all.

He was surprised by the frequency with which this experience occurs and suggested that his own research raises the question as to how something so common can be so unknown.

From my perspective without a biblical worldview or reference point, Hufford is not quite sure what to make of his own findings. Although he would give place to the possibility that these night terror experiences argue for a metaphysical reality, he concludes that "the state in which this experience occurs is probably best described as sleep paralysis with a particular kind of hypnagogic hallucination."

I would agree with Hufford's hypothesis attributing some of these experiences to a known psycho-physiological state. However, without taking into account the reality of the spiritual world, his conclusions are incomplete.

In their book, ***The Seduction of Our Children***, Dr. Neil Anderson and Steve Russo give us another perspective (pages 26-36).

"I was conducting a conference for the leadership of one of America's flagship churches. The pastor is one of the most gifted Bible teachers I know, and his staff is among the best. I asked the 165 leaders present if they had ever experienced a direct encounter with something they knew to be demonic, such as a frightening presence in their room or an evil voice in their mind. Ninety-five percent answered yes.

I went a step further to ask how many had been frightened by something pressing on them that they couldn't immediately respond to physically. At least a third raised their hand. Are these Christian leaders mentally ill? No, and neither are your children when they struggle against demonic influences in their lives. Would you know what to do if your child was terrorized by a presence in his room? Do you fear such a possibility?"

In this same book, Anderson and Russo record the results of a survey of 1725 students (433 junior high and 1292 senior high) who attended Christian schools and camps. Half of the junior high and 47% of the senior high students said that they had experienced a frightening presence in their room. Even among the 864 students who indicated no occult background whatsoever the frequency of experiencing such a presence was still 40%.

In 1992 Kathy and I conducted a comparable survey in Miami, Florida at the Christian school where she was a fourth grade teacher. We surveyed 92 junior high and 122 senior high students. One of the questions we asked was, "Have you ever experienced some presence (seen or heard) in your room that scared you?" Our results were remarkably similar to those cited above, as 46% of the junior high students and 47% of the senior high students responded that they had.

In order to understand such occurrences as well as wage and win such spiritual battles, we need to see the world the way God sees it. We need a biblical *worldview* that includes a healthy, balanced understanding of the spiritual realm.

In our western culture, we have tended to believe that only what we can observe with our five senses or understand scientifically is what is real. This rational, materialistic (dealing with the material or physical world) worldview is in direct opposition to biblical Christianity which says "for we walk [live] by faith and not by sight" (2 Corinthians 5:7). Biblical Christianity makes it clear that beyond the physical universe there is a very real and very much active spiritual world that includes not only God Himself but spiritual beings called angels and demons.

Some "mind science" cult groups go to the opposite extreme. They say that the physical world is illusory and only that which is of the mind or spirit is real. The problem with their worldview is that it is kind of like Grape Nuts™ cereal. Grape Nuts is neither grapes nor nuts. These cult groups are neither Christian nor science!

A truly biblical worldview allows for the "seen" world of God's natural creation as well as the "unseen" world of God Himself and the spirit world of angels and demons. The apostle Paul did not deny the existence of the material world when he wrote, "for the things which are seen are temporal, but the things which are not seen are eternal" (2 Corinthians 4:18). He was simply pointing out the fact that what we can observe with our senses today will not be around forever.

Dr. Neil Anderson and Dr. Timothy Warner clearly explained and illustrated this biblical worldview in their book, *Beginner's Guide to Spiritual Warfare,* (page 69):

> "Biblical worldview has three functional realms: the realm of God or deity, the realm of angels and the realm of people and things. It is important to state that when we talk about these realms, we are not talking about spatial realms but realms of being. God is certainly not limited to a spatial realm far away in outer space. He is present everywhere in his creation. But God is the one being in the realm of deity, not God and angels, and certainly not God and Satan. Some Christians have such a fear of Satan that they ascribe godlike qualities to him. Some have even confessed that they see him as the counterpart of God. God being the eternal good and Satan the eternal evil. Satan isn't the eternal anything. He is a fallen angel and should never have the attributes of deity ascribed to him."

It is not necessary here to examine and try to understand the origin of the spirit world of angels and demons. Scripture doesn't answer all our questions on this matter anyway. What is clear is that angels and demons are created, spirit beings and therefore do not have physical bodies as we do. However, they play an important role in what takes place in real time-space history on planet earth.

Remember, He, the Holy Spirit who lives in us is greater than he, the devil, who lives in the world (1 John 4:4). Jesus came to destroy the works of the devil (1 John 3:8) and has already disarmed him through the Cross (Colossians 2:15-16).

In the Bible, angels worship God (Revelation 5:11-12), execute God's judgments on earth, (Revelation 8 & 9), and bring important messages to people. An angel appeared to Zacharias, father of John the Baptist and gave a verbal message to him (Luke 1:11-20). Mary, the mother of Jesus also received an angelic visitation (Luke 1:26-38), as did her husband, Joseph, though his visitation was in the form of a dream (Matthew 1:20-25).

Although visual appearances of angels are not commonplace, Scripture indicates that they may be ministering to us far more often than we realize. Hebrews 1:14, speaking of angels states, "Are they not all ministering spirits, sent out to render service for the sake of those who will inherit salvation?" Apparently angels, <u>never demons,</u> also have the capacity to assume human form at times, for later in Hebrews it reads, "Do not neglect to show hospitality to strangers, for by this some have entertained angels without knowing it" (Hebrews 13:2). The following diagram is worth a thousand words in understanding the world from a biblical point of view:

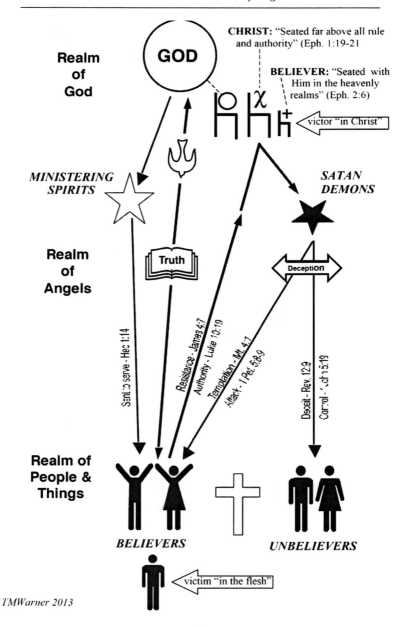

We are not to worship angels (Revelation 19:10, 22:8-9) though seeing them in their glory and authority as John did in this vision must be truly awe-inspiring. God's holy angels are certainly not plump little pink-cheeked babies flitting around plucking harps! They are grand, majestic beings that are immensely powerful in strength and voice, far greater than any man or demon. Here's just one example from Revelation 10:1-3:

> *"I saw another strong angel coming down out of heaven, clothed with a cloud; and the rainbow was upon his head, and his face was like the sun, and his feet like pillars of fire; and he had in his hand a little book which was open. He placed his right foot on the sea and his left foot on the land; and he cried out with a loud voice, as when a lion roars; and when he had cried out, the seven peals of thunder uttered their voices."*

There is one more function of angels that is especially pertinent to this book. They are mighty warriors, fighting against Satan and his forces engaged in a cosmic war for the hearts of men and the souls of nations, (Daniel 10 and Revelation 12:1-9),

So what about demons? What are they?

Demons are by nature cruel liars and deceivers. Jesus unmasked the enemy while rebuking the unrepentant Pharisees when He said:

> *"You are of your father the devil, and you want to do the desires of your father. He was a murderer from the beginning, and does not stand in the truth because there is no truth in him. Whenever he speaks a lie, he speaks from his own nature, for he is a liar and the father of lies."* (John 8:44).

Satan and his forces (demons) want to make good things appear bad and bad things appear good, so that we'll reject the good and receive the bad. When tempting Eve in the Garden of Eden, he attacked God's goodness, slandering the truthfulness of His character. In response to God's promise that eating from the tree of the knowledge of good and evil would result in death (Genesis 2:17), the devil declared in Genesis 3:4-5:

> *"You surely will not die! For God knows that in the day you eat from it your eyes will be opened, and you will be like God, knowing good and evil."*

The devil's insinuations were clear: You can't trust God. God is just looking out for Himself. He doesn't want you to experience all the good things in life, because He wants to keep you under His thumb. In this case, hindsight is 20/20. The devil was clearly lying but Adam & Eve didn't see it.

Much of spiritual battle is won or lost on this very battlefield... the battlefield of our beliefs about God. What we believe or disbelieve about God is the most important thing about us, and it really is a battle for our minds. However, if what you believe isn't true, then how you feel will not reflect biblical reality. How many of you reading this book about spiritual warfare have memorized Philippians 4:8 to know how to take every thought captive to the obedience of Christ (2 Cor. 10:3-5)?

Do we truly trust that God loves us and is good and wants the best for us, even when life on this fallen planet hands us a raw deal? The devil and his forces will work overtime to convince us faith in God is a waste of time.

Make no mistake. The powers of darkness hate God with a passion and so have unleashed a ferocious "no holds barred" assault on His most treasured creation, mankind. Demonic forces are hard at work trying to whisper lies into our minds to distort our picture of God. They will use any and all resources at their disposal, including false religions, deceived people, ungodly media (books, movies, computer and video games, music, pornography, news media, etc.) and even direct communication into our minds to try and implant their lies into our thinking. Have you ever battled with one or more of these images of God?

Rich Miller, President of Freedom in Christ Ministries, suggests the following:

- God is so distant and disinterested and busy with running planet earth, He really doesn't have time for me. It's not really possible to have a close relationship with Him. He loves everybody, I guess, but deep down He really doesn't love *me*.

- God is severe and stern. Maybe even cruel and abusive. He doesn't want us to have fun here on earth and He frowns on those who enjoy life "too much."

- The only way to please God is rigorously keep His commands. He is quick to notice when we fail and even quicker to bring punishment. He loves us when we're good, but is very angry with us when we're not.

- God doesn't expect us to be perfect. He knows we all have vices and is kind of like a kindly, old grandfather. God winks and looks the other way at our sin.

- There are many ways to God. All religions are basically the same. It doesn't matter which one you choose, just so you are sincere.

Each one of these pictures of God is a distortion. If you have believed any of them, you have been deceived by the father of lies. Scripture reveals God's character to be "gracious and merciful, slow to anger and great in loving kindness" (Psalm 145:8). He is not distant and unreachable for Isaiah 55:6-7 invites us to "Seek the Lord while He may be found; call upon Him while He is near. Let the wicked forsake His way and the unrighteous man his thoughts; and let him return to the LORD, and He will have compassion on him, and to our God, for He will abundantly pardon."

The way back to God is not complicated nor confusing. It is simply through repentance and forgiveness.

He Himself said, "I am the way and the truth and the life; no one comes to the Father but through Me" (John 14:6).

The gospel or good news is simple. God loves us. All of us have sinned and that sin separates us from God and His love. Jesus died and thus paid the penalty required by God for our sin. Jesus rose from the dead and now offers us forgiveness of sin and a new life. When we confess our sin and need for Jesus' cleansing and open our hearts by faith to receive Him, He becomes the Leader (Lord) and Forgiver (Savior) of our lives.

Our forgiveness and relationship with God does not come through working hard to keep God's commands. That is impossible, for all of us have failed to measure up to His standard of perfect righteousness. But when we, by faith, receive God's free gift of forgiveness in Christ, the perfect righteousness of Jesus is credited to us!

If you have never begun the most important relationship of your life, a rich, warm Father-child relationship with our loving God, provided through His Son, Jesus Christ, we want to give you that opportunity right now. If the Lord has opened your eyes and heart so you see your need for forgiveness and new life through Christ, we heartily welcome you to pray along with us:

> *Dear heavenly Father, I come to You with nothing to offer except my own sin and my need for You to be merciful to me. I know that all my efforts to earn a place in Your family fall flat before Your holy, perfect righteousness. In my helplessness to save myself, I look to Jesus alone to forgive and cleanse me. Thank*

You for His death on the cross that was the full payment for my sins. Thank You that because He rose from the dead, He can give me new life, His life. I renounce any and all allegiance to the ways and works of darkness and I pledge allegiance to the Lord Jesus alone. I receive Him and by Your promise, Father, now gratefully take my place in Your family as Your child, holy and dearly loved. Thank You for being merciful to me and saving me this day. In Jesus' powerful Name I pray, amen.

If you made that decision to receive Christ, welcome to the family of God! You have made the most important decision of your life and we encourage you to share what you've done with another Christian you know and trust. He or she can help you begin growing in your faith. In addition, you are going to find the rest of this book very helpful in your new found faith, especially the next chapter!

As vitally important as Jesus' saving us from sin is, it is not the whole story. He also came to deliver (rescue) us from the devil's rule in our lives. Christ accomplished that through His death, burial and resurrection.

Now that Jesus has utterly defeated sin, death and the devil, we can (through Christ), learn to win the daily battles against the schemes of the enemy. And that's what the rest of this book is all about.

You might still be wondering about that evil presence that haunted me earlier in my life. It no longer concerns me because I know who I am in Christ and how to repel such an attack. Had I known Christ then as I know Him now, I could have simply followed James 4:7 which says, "Submit therefore to God. Resist the devil and he will flee from you." In my heart I would have surrendered to God's Lordship in my life and then verbally I would have told that thing to "Go, in Jesus name!" And it would've been all over.

Sound too simple? Well, there's a lot more that goes along with being able to stand against the enemy so authoritatively. Remember, we've just begun our boot camp training for spiritual battle. The battle plan is not fully in place yet. We've looked briefly at who God is and how to be rightly related to Him in this chapter. And we've caught a quick glimpse of our victorious Jesus. In the next chapter we'll learn more about our identity and position in Christ and how that opens the door for joining Him in His victory. Prepare to be encouraged!

Dear heavenly Father, what a good and true and holy and loving and faithful and merciful and powerful God You are! Despite all the lies about You that the devil has tried to get me to believe, I drive a stake in the ground right now and declare that I will trust in You no matter what. I have known that Your ways are different than mine and at times I have been angry because You did not do things my way. But now I know that Your ways are higher than mine (Isaiah 55:9) and it should not surprise me when I do not fully grasp Your purposes. Instead of rebelling, I choose to rest in You. Instead of whining, I choose to worship. Instead of trying to make my own way, I choose to trust. Make straight paths for my feet, Lord, as I journey ahead, walking with You and waging the battle and by Your grace, winning. In Jesus Name I pray, Amen.

Chapter Four

The Boy Becomes a Warrior

It was a cold February morning in 1968. America was rapidly deploying more troops into the Vietnam conflict and the military draft was in full swing. Born in 1949, my choices in 1967 after high school graduation and dropping out of college I was faced with being drafted. So, wanting a few more options than the 2 million others who were drafted for two years, I made the choice to enlist for three years that gave me some options other than being an infantry soldier.

I enlisted in the Army at the Elgin, Illinois recruiting center, and then went on for processing. It was a full day of physical exams and aptitude tests designed to see if I qualified. At the end of the day they declared me fit for service. All of us who passed the tests were sworn in that afternoon.

A few weeks later I would be heading off to basic training or, as it was officially titled, "Initial Entry Training." Everyone else called it "boot camp."

The Boy Becomes a Warrior

I was assigned to go through eight weeks of basic training at the Army base in Fort Leonard Wood, Missouri. Boot camp can be a scary experience. It was designed as a mind game to tear down our civilian self-identity and replace it with a corporate military one. We were only allowed to bring one suitcase with specifically designated items of clothing and toiletries. You didn't dare bring anything more to boot camp than what was allowed.

I had said my farewells to my family the night before I left. The next morning my father dropped me off at the departure station. We hugged each other and said good-bye. From his experience in World War II he knew what I was headed for, though I didn't. I will always remember the look on his face as I stepped onto that bus. He was sending his firstborn son to fight for freedom, freedoms that we enjoyed as a nation and which were now in jeopardy in a country 12,000 miles away. He knew it might mean laying down my life, and never seeing me alive again.

This was one of the loneliest times of my life. I think I saw tears running down my father's cheeks that day as he walked away from the bus. I will never fully understand what it cost my father that day, but I was glad he was there with me.

After two months of basic training I then spent several months at Ft. Eustis, VA to become a helicopter crew chief. While there I was accepted into flight school that was a nine month training program and became a helicopter pilot. Once I graduated in 1969 I was given orders for Vietnam.

I will spare you the tiresome details of boot camp. It was repetitious, very demanding and at times humiliating.

There was nothing glamorous about it though there was a significant measure of satisfaction in having made it through. A large portion of our time was taken up with marching, drill ceremonies, lots of standing very still in formations, running, pushups, shooting, physical and emotional training (including being yelled at a lot!), discipline to detail, and learning how to use our weapons to defeat the enemy.

The goal was not so much to train us to be killers as it was to teach us to work as a team in order to accomplish a mission. The mission as we knew it was to help the helpless and make sure each team member came back alive. Where the enemy stood in the way, he would have to be removed.

Both the Marines and the Army have distinct ways of bringing boot camp to a close. It is a 72 hour marathon of food and sleep deprivation, marching and training exercises. The Marines call it "The Crucible." The Army at Fort Jackson, SC calls their event, "Victory Forge", and all other Army basic training sites have something similar.

In a Department of Defense (DOD) article describing the transformation that takes place through basic training, one Marine stated:

> *"We are not just giving them basic training, we're turning them into Marines. There is more to being a Marine than knowing how to fire a weapon. There is an entire tradition behind it, and we want these recruits to measure up to the men and women who went before them."*

Commenting on the U.S. Army's culmination of basic training, General John A. Van Alstyne of Fort Jackson said:

> *"Soldiers now feel like they are pushed both physically and mentally, and they are proud of what they have done. Training companies routinely come out of Victor Forge looking like rifle platoons that just finished two days of combat operations. When the drill sergeants walk down the line and congratulate the soldiers, telling them that they have done a good job, many of them break down and cry. They are being told this by someone they really respect. It means a lot to them."*

Victory Forge ends at night, and soldiers gather around a fiery forge. As the flames shoot out of the pit, the battalion commander puts their basic training experiences into perspective. He holds up a steel rod and tells them that they came to boot camp with much potential, but yet unshaped. But now completing their initiation into the Army by finishing this last test course in basic training, he symbolically drops the steel rod and reaches into the forge and pulls out a fine-tooled sword.

Up until that moment, the men and women are called "recruits." But as the commander pulls out the sword from the flames, for the first time he calls them "soldiers." They have made it, they truly belong and now they really know it! The relief, joy and satisfaction are overwhelming as those words of affirmation are spoken.

How many of God's people are living life trying desperately to "make it," to gain some kind of assurance that they truly belong to God's family and are accepted by Him and acceptable to Him? To be able to hear one clear word of affirmation from the Father's heart that they are loved and lovable would bring them immeasurable relief, unquenchable joy, and incredible satisfaction of soul.

Perhaps that is you today. You know God is *supposed* to love you, because the Bible says He loves everybody, right? You can quote John 3:16 backwards and forwards and yet whatever love you sense from the Father seems locked in your head, unable to resonate in your heart.

We wish we could toss a spiritual hand grenade and blast away any wall of guilt, shame, unworthiness, bitterness or unbelief that blocks God's truth from entering into your heart, but we can't. You must do that for yourself as you reject any lies you've believed, embrace God's truth, confess any sins you've committed and forgive all who have hurt you. We are praying as you read this book that God will bring a breakthrough in your life that will enable you to shout your "Amen!" to the truth that,

> *"...you have not received a spirit of slavery leading to fear again, but you have received a spirit of adoption as sons by which we cry out, Abba-Father! The Spirit Himself testifies with our spirit that we are children of God"* (Romans 8:15-16).

This is supremely important. In order for us to wage war as victorious soldiers of Christ, we must first know that we are dearly loved children of God. Only that rock solid assurance of our right standing with God and His deep delight in us will give us the security of soul to effectively engage the enemy in battle.

You cannot be strong in the Lord if you do not know what it means to be "in the Lord." That's the whole theme of Ephesians chapter one. In Christ, or in union with Him, we are saints, blessed with every spiritual blessing, chosen by Him to be holy, lovingly adopted by Him in kindness, lavishly given His grace, accepted, redeemed, forgiven, given a wonderful inheritance (see Ephesians 1:1-12)! And He sealed the whole deal by giving us the Holy Spirit of promise (Ephesians 1:13-14).

Are you beginning to get the message that you are not a *recruit* but a treasured child of God hand-picked to serve in the greatest army there ever was, the army of King Jesus!

We have the assurance that He is "able to do far more abundantly beyond all that we ask or think, according to the power that works within us" (Ephesians 3:20)!

We cannot say this anymore passionately. If you have trusted Christ alone to save you from your sins, then you're in! You belong! You are accepted and acceptable to God. You are a member in good standing of the Father's family and He loves you as He loves His Son, Jesus!

Many times we feel utterly unworthy of such lavish, affectionate love from God because we know how often and how awfully we can sin. But God's love for us does not fluctuate like the Dow Jones industrial average. It is not based on how well or poorly we performed spiritually today, yesterday or any day. It is based on the unchanging nature of God (see James 1:17), and God's nature is to love because God is love (1 John 4:15-17).

At this point many believers in Christ are still unsure. They have heard Jeremiah 17:9 that says, "the heart is more deceitful than all else and is desperately sick," and if their heart is like that, how could God possibly love them?

Let's set the record straight. Jeremiah's description of the human heart is accurate for someone without Christ, but it is not meant to be a diagnosis of the heart of a new covenant follower of Jesus. Ezekiel 36:25-28 describes what happens when we turn to the Lord:

> *"Then I [God] will sprinkle clean water on you, and you will be clean; I will cleanse you from all your filthiness and from all your idols. Moreover, I will give you a new heart and put a new spirit within you; and I will remove the heart of stone from your flesh and give you a heart of flesh. I will put My Spirit within you and cause you to walk in My statutes, and you will be careful to observe My ordinances."*

Every believer in Christ, at the moment of salvation, is transformed into an entirely new person. We are given a new, soft heart. We are given a new, alive spirit. And the Holy Spirit comes to live within us so that our bodies are called "a temple of the Holy Spirit" (1 Corinthians 6:19). You could not ask for greater dignity to be granted to your body than for God Himself to make it His home!

Second Corinthians 5:17 says, "Therefore if anyone is in Christ, he is a new creature; the old things passed away; behold, new things have come." In reality, Christians are a whole new species of humanity that has never existed before, for we are people that have the living presence of the Living Christ, dwelling Spirit-to-spirit with us!

Under the old covenant (old testament), the Spirit of God would come *upon* people (kings, prophets, etc.) for the purpose of service. In Christ, the Spirit of God has come to dwell *within* people for the purpose of transformation from the inside out.

One of the devil's favorite lies he tells to Christians is to make them think that deep down they are really the same person they always were; they just happen to be going to heaven now.

That's why it really upsets us when we hear people saying, "Oh, I'm just a wicked old sinner saved by grace." In essence they're saying, "I'm nothing, nothing, nothing. I'm just the dirt under the little toenail of the body of Christ."

Give us a break! That's not you at all! You *were* a wicked old sinner but you *have been* saved by grace and now you *are* a saint, a holy one! A saint who still sins, to be sure, but a saint nonetheless! Sainthood doesn't mean perfection. It just means that we have been transferred from the kingdom of darkness into God's marvelous Kingdom of Light.

Don't believe us? Then believe the apostle Paul! All through his letters, he greets the believers, calling them *saints*. Even the Corinthian church, whose behavior was often not very saintly, was greeted as follows:

> *"To the church of God which is at Corinth, to those who have been sanctified in Christ Jesus, saints by calling, with all who in every place call on the name of our Lord Jesus Christ, their Lord and ours: Grace to you and peace from God our Father and the Lord Jesus Christ"* (1 Corinthians 1:2-3).

My religious background painted a wrong picture of a saint. Growing up, a saint to me was a statue I prayed to, a super-spiritual person who performed miracles and who was, years and years later, declared to be a "saint" by the church. In other words, I knew I was not and would likely never be, a saint. But in Christ, I am now Saint Joseph! So the next time you're wearing a name tag put a "St." in front of your name. Just don't put it after your name or you become a street ☺

If we are saints, then why is sin still a problem? After all, Romans 6:1-7 makes it clear that we are dead to sin and alive to God. But being dead to sin does not mean we are incapable of sinning. It means sin no longer holds tyrannical control over our lives. We can now choose righteousness instead of unrighteousness. As Ephesians 4:20-32 teaches, we must now choose to "lay aside" the old self and its practices and "put on" the new. As Christians we are now faced with just two choices every day: to walk according to the flesh (self-sufficiency without Christ's strength) or walk by faith in the power of the Holy Spirit, doing things God's way (Galatians 5:13-18).

In essence, though we have been rescued from the gutter and adopted into God's royal family and given a whole, new clean wardrobe, we still have a choice to make. We can get up in the morning, go in the closet, pull out and put on those new, sharp-looking garments, or we can put on those old, filthy rags lying in a heap on the floor. And sadly, sometimes we do just that. After all, though they look and smell bad and are not indicative of our new identity, they are familiar and we know how to act in them.

Such is the lure of sin. It promises a measure of pleasure and familiarity. On the other hand, it takes a step of faith to begin to walk around in the garments of righteousness we have in Christ. And faith can seem risky until you truly get to know the One who holds your hand.

The new covenant (new testament) call to righteous living is based on who we have now become in Christ, new creations! Paul wrote, "Therefore I, the prisoner of the Lord, implore you to walk in a manner worthy of the calling with which you have been called" (Ephesians 4:1).

It is the call for the slave of sin who has been set free to be a slave to righteousness instead (Romans 6:20-22). It is the call for the one rescued from the domain of darkness to now walk as a child of the light (Colossians 1:13; Ephesians 5:6-10). It is the call for those who were dead in sin but have been brought to life to walk in newness of life (Ephesians 2:1-5; Romans 6:4). It is the call for the one who was once a helpless POW in the enemy's cruel concentration camp to fight the good fight as a good soldier of Christ Jesus (2 Timothy 2:3-7). As the apostle Paul wrote so poignantly:

> *"For when you were slaves of sin, you were free in regard to righteousness. Therefore what benefit were you then*

> *deriving from the things of which you are now ashamed? For the outcome of those things is death. But now having been freed from sin and enslaved to God, you derive your benefit, resulting in sanctification, and the outcome, eternal life."* (Romans 6:20-22)

Sin is a liar. It never delivers what it promises, and what it ends up delivering is a heart that becomes increasingly hard (Hebrews 3:12-13). When we give into sin, we deny the reality of who we are and what we were made for in Christ, and in actuality, we declare civil war against our own bodies. First Peter 2:9-11 sums this up powerfully:

> *"But you are a chosen race, a royal priesthood, a holy nation, a people for God's own possession, so that you may proclaim the excellencies of Him who has called you out of darkness into His marvelous light; for once you were not a people, but now you are the people of God; you had not received mercy, but now you have received mercy. Beloved, I urge you as aliens and strangers to abstain from fleshly lusts which wage war against your soul."*

When a man or woman becomes a soldier, there is a long legacy of valiant warriors and courageous heroes in whose boot steps you must follow. And he or she is proud to do it. It has been a high honor and responsibility to guard the tradition of serving my fellow soldiers.

John Eldridge in his book, ***Waking the Dead*** (p.17), describes our spiritual battle so well when he said:

> *"Until we come to terms with war as the context of our days, we will not understand life. We will misinterpret ninety percent of what is happening around us and to us...You won't understand your life, you won't see clearly what has happened to you or how you live forward from here, unless you see it as a battle. A war against your heart."*

Chapter Five
Armed and Dangerous

The sun seemed to pause for a moment on the horizon before launching into another scorching day in the tropics of Southeast Asia as we cranked the turbine engines on our helicopters. It was one of those tranquil moments to get lost in as my rotor blades turned at flight idle. My nineteen year old mind mercifully took a mini reprieve away from the intensity of life in a war zone and what we were about to face. I was an aircraft commander of a Huey helicopter. Snapping me back to reality, a voice crackled through the earphones in my flight helmet:

"Cu Chi Tower, Cu Chi Tower, this is Little Bear Six in the Bear Pit with seven slicks and two Stingers in the Hornet's Nest for take-off."

In response the air traffic controller fired back instructions, as there were literally scores of other pilots requesting taxiing and take-off clearance to fly a variety of missions. Our turbine engines were now at full speed. Whether it was reconnaissance, re-supply, air support, medical evacuation (medevac), or combat assault, daybreak signaled another day to engage the enemy. Today our unit would fly another combat assault mission. In flight formation we all came to a hover as the tower operator said, "Roger, Little Bear Six, you are cleared to go out runway 24. Contact air traffic control and Cu Chi artillery before clearing the perimeter."

We moved to the active runway, ready to take off in flight formation. Training, precision, planning and vigilance were essential, not only for flight safety and insertion of troops into the LZ, but for the overall success of the mission.

"Stingers" were gunship helicopters used for attack support. Each "slick" or UH-1H helicopter was loaded with a four-man crew: two pilots (like myself) up front, our crew chief and door gunner who were strapped into the rear of the chopper in their wells behind their mounted M60 machine guns. Space and weight limitations allowed us to carry only six infantrymen, each carrying rug sacks upwards of 80-90 pounds of ammunition, water and supplies.

We swiftly moved down the runway as we prepared to engage the enemy again. Each pilot monitored three to four different radio frequencies at any given time. This was as difficult to master as flying the aircraft itself. On take-off, the crew chief and door gunner (sitting on opposite sides of the helicopter) would let the pilots know via the intercom if we were getting dangerously close to other helicopters in our formation. There was also communication with all other helicopters, including the gunships flying alongside of us and sometimes with the F-4 fighter pilots we called "fast movers" who were out in front of us to drop their napalm and other ordinance around the LZ, clearing the way before we landed.

As we gained altitude and airspeed before clearing the base camp perimeter, we all monitored Cu Chi's artillery frequency. There were numerous artillery batteries placed at strategic locations around the base camp which fired into our LZ and other targets. To fly in front of them was to risk being shot down by friendly fire. Once clear of the base camp, Little Bear Six, the call sign for the Command and Control helicopter (flying higher and out in front of us), would direct our assault into the LZ.

Climbing quickly to 1500 ft., we were effectively out of range of small arms fire. There were no cargo doors on our aircraft, and as the 100 knot wind blew through our open troop compartment, it provided temporary relief from the oppressive jungle heat below.

We were rapidly approaching the LZ. From high above, Little Bear Six ordered us to drop down to knap of the earth. Everyone tensed up. There was no way of knowing what kind of situation we might encounter.

The artillery was already pounding the LZ with 105mm shells. On our flank was a forward air controller marking targets for the F-4 Phantom pilots, who flashed by us screaming upward after dropping their napalm loads. Helicopter gunships went into their race track pattern on either side of the formation providing us with rocket and machine gun cover fire around the perimeters of the LZ.

I gave the order to the door gunners to lay down suppressive fire into the tree line surrounding the LZ as we landed. All of the pilots flared the noses of our birds in unison, carefully feeling for the ground below us. The infantrymen (or "grunts") didn't wait for us to touch down. They had already spotted the muzzle flashes from AK-47 automatic weapon fire from the enemy. Men were screaming and guns were firing. It was a "hot" LZ. The grunts jumped out both sides of the helicopter and moved quickly into combat formation to engage the enemy.

Men had already been wounded and the medics on the ground were doing everything they could to apply field dressings to stop the bleeding and prevent loss of life. Other soldiers who were unwounded leaned heavily into the firefight. A couple of our slicks who had just cleared the tree line stayed at low level, out of enemy sight. I made a quick 180 degree turn and headed back into the teeth of the battle to extract the wounded. It would take too long for the medevac choppers to arrive. We had to do it ourselves.

The gunships above were running low on fuel and ammunition and would soon need to return to base camp to rearm and refuel. Our slicks could return quickly with reinforcements and supplies if needed, extract our troops if they were heavily outnumbered or when the battle was over.

The platoon commander on the ground called the artillery and air support units to adjust their fire support to the front of the assault. Maps of the area had to be read accurately and quickly. One small mistake could have resulted in their dropping a shell into the middle of our own troops. Trust between infantrymen, artillery and air support was vital, as radio operators coordinated the adjustment in weapons fire. Soon both the artillery and air support firepower were swishing safely overhead of our troops, exploding into the enemy's position.

To those in Washington, DC and Hanoi, North Vietnam this was just one of many combat assaults, but to those on the ground and to those of us providing air support, the stakes were much higher. The battle had just begun and it was a life or death situation.

Were we ever anxious, nervous or even afraid going into these battles? Of course we were, but we were compelled to do our job anyway. Courage is not the absence of fear; it is doing what is right and necessary even in the face of fear. Every time we went out on a mission, there was the possibility we might not return whole or even alive, but we did not and could not allow those thoughts to control us. Besides, on the other side of the "ledger" we had a few things going for us.

First, we had already received the best training possible. Second, we had state of the art weapons and technical equipment. Third, we had experiences of success under our belts. Fourth, we had each other.

In the spiritual battles some of our brothers and sisters in Christ around the world experience this as a life or death situation the same way we did in Vietnam. In some countries imprisonments, beatings, tortures and even death await those who convert to Christianity or attempt to bring others to faith in Christ.

In the U.S., at least at the present time, the risks are not as great. When we share the gospel here we might experience someone sighing or rolling their eyeballs in disinterest. We might experience shunning by a fellow employee or classmate, or even the rejection of a family member or friend. Those occurrences are painful, no doubt about it, but they are certainly not life threatening.

Unfortunately, most of us never get to the point of knowing how the other person might respond to the Gospel because we lose the spiritual battle for our minds before that even happens. The anxiety, nervousness and fear we experience in anticipation of sharing the good news steals our joy, kills our enthusiasm and destroys our will to reach out. And sadly, instead of "running to the battle lines" like David did with Goliath (1 Samuel 17:22), we grab a snack and turn on the TV.

Whenever we were headed out to a hostile and dangerous LZ we knew what we had to do in order to accomplish the mission because we had been well-trained and well-armed. We were equipped with the best the U.S. Army had to offer at that time. Sometimes a large part of the battle for our minds can be won by getting some basic training in how to share our faith. Talk to your pastor or a spiritual mentor about your desire to get practical, relational training on how to share your faith. It's amazing how much boldness we develop when we know what to do and say as we are empowered by the Holy Spirit to do it!

As a chopper pilot in the Army I was equipped with a 40lb armored "chicken plate" that fit over my chest under the shoulder harness in my seat and protected my chest and abdomen. The flight seat itself was also armor plated, protecting the rest of my body. I carried a loaded firearm which I used on occasion when under attack. We were not invulnerable by any stretch of the imagination, but with the technology to defend ourselves and the weapons to attack with precision and power in our helicopters we were armed and dangerous.

Child of God, do you know that in Christ we are armed and dangerous, too? No, we don't fight with napalm or artillery shells or even nuclear weapons. But, when it comes to spiritual battle, God has outfitted us with spiritual weapons of great power. Consider these Scriptures:

> **"For though we live in the world, we do not wage war as the world does. The weapons we fight with are not the weapons of the world. On the contrary, they have divine power to demolish strongholds. We demolish arguments and every pretension that sets itself up against the knowledge of God, and we take captive every thought to make it obedient to Christ" (2 Corinthians 10:3-5).**
>
> **"For our struggle is not against flesh and blood, but against the rulers, against the powers, against the world forces of this darkness, against the spiritual forces of wickedness in the heavenly places. Therefore, take up the full armor of God, so that you will be able to resist in the evil day, and having done everything, to stand firm. Stand firm, therefore, having girded your loins with truth, and having put on the breastplate of righteousness, and having shod your feet with the preparation of the gospel of peace; in addition to all, taking up the shield of faith with**

which you will be able to extinguish all the flaming arrows of the evil one. And take up the helmet of salvation, and the sword of the Spirit, which is the word God" (Ephesians 6:12-17).

Whoever heard of fighting a war with things like kindness and love? Well, it shouldn't surprise us as God's weapons are different than man's!

The bottom line in all spiritual warfare is a battle for the glory of God. Dr. Timothy Warner explained this battle for glory when he wrote in his book, *Spiritual Warfare* (p.40):

> *"If glory is the issue at stake, why don't we talk about a glory encounter rather than a power encounter? There is a very good reason for this. Satan cannot compete at the level of glory. Any aspects about him which are or were glorious came from a reflected glory and not from any quality of his own. The glory of God, however, derives from qualities in His very nature and thus depends on no source higher or other than Himself. His creative and sustaining power evidenced in our universe and taken as a whole begins to define God's glory. At best Satan's acts are deceptive shows of power or counterfeits of God's mighty acts in order to impress and lead astray a people whose perceptions have been badly distorted by sin."*

The devil and his demons don't want God to look good and they will try to defame His name by making you look bad. So, as you look at the battles you are facing whether it is the strong temptation to do evil, the attacks of guilt, shame, fear or anxiety of the enemy, the deception of materialism and the love of stuff, ask the Lord to show you how to fight... *for His glory!*

As you step out in faith and watch God come through, your faith and confidence in Him and in His using you will grow. And when you fail, you will experience His grace to sustain you and motivate you to continue the battle. And you will learn to be a good soldier of Christ Jesus.

One final word: The commands to "put on the full armor of God" were not given to an individual. They were written to a church, a group of believers loving each other and battling for each other. True, each individual has the responsibility to personally choose truth, walk in righteousness, etc., but we are not in this battle alone. We have each other.

> *Dear heavenly Father, You have said, "Do not be overcome by evil, but overcome evil with good" (Romans 12:21). Please empower me by the Holy Spirit to put on the full armor of God and use the weapons You've given me in Christ. I want to be well-trained with love, patience, kindness, humility, purity, praise and worship, prayer and fasting, truth, righteousness, peace, the proclamation of the gospel, faith, salvation and Your word to resist,*

stand firm and fight the spiritual battles in and around me. Connect me with other like-minded brothers and sisters in Christ so we can lock arms and armor together. Thank You that since Jesus has already won the war, together we can win the battles in Your kingdom, by Your power and for Your glory. In Jesus' name, A men.

Chapter Six

The Unseen Hand

Much of the Vietnam war took place under cover of night because the enemy could hide behind the veil of darkness and not be spotted from the air as they pushed supplies and men along the Ho Chi Minh trail from Cambodia into Vietnam. In response to this, the U.S. Army sent out ambush patrols, hoping to catch enemy troop movements by surprise.

Every ambush patrol had a different radio frequency. We would check in with all of them at designated times as we flew high above their positions from a safe altitude. We were like a mother hen spreading her wings over her "chicks" in order to protect them. However, we needed to be careful how we communicated with them so as not to compromise their location with too much radio chatter. Each soldier on the ground was typically hunkered down in a foxhole quickly dug in after dark, once they reached their night positions.

I was flying what was called a single ship "Night Hawk" gunship. There was a mini-gun mounted on the

The Unseen Hand

left of the helicopter behind my seat that could fire 4,000 rounds a minute. We also had a million candle power spot light mounted in the back well behind the mini-gun. On the right side of the aircraft we had a huge bucket of flares in a basket hanging out the ride side of the cargo bay. These were very large flares. We could only carry ten of them because of their size and weight. They each had a cable attached to the detonator that we would hook to a D-Ring on the floor of the cargo bay floor. Whenever a flare was tossed out the door the cable was pulled and soon it would explode underneath us and slowly ride to the ground on a parachute. We dropped these from 3,000 ft. altitude. They would light up the target area underneath us like it was daytime. We would then dive down and get underneath the flare and give covering fire to the six man ambush patrol we were protecting. This was always a very "sporty" proposition. One of the soldiers had a strobe light in his helmet so that we knew their position when we opened up the mini gun within yards of their position. It was clear to us vertically but could not be seen horizontally by the enemy.

Many times the enemy would send only a few soldiers down a trail or river, scouting out the strength of our resistance before moving in with their larger force. Once the position of our ambush patrols was compromised, the rest of the enemy forces would swarm in and try to overrun them.

This November night in 1969 was quieter than most. We were flying high above the battle field making our rounds over numerous ambush patrols scattered across rice paddies, jungle trails and rivers. We were briefed in the TOC Command Center (tactical operation's center) at dusk every night before taking off. Each one had their own unique radio frequency and we marked them on our maps strapped to our legs with their grid coordinates.

We returned to base camp for refueling so we could then go back out for further surveillance. As we sat on the landing pad in the refueling area, our engine on (always hot refueling) and our rotor blades turning at flight idle an urgent call came in over the radio, desperate for help. The soldiers were under heavy fire and needed to be resupplied. Their ammunition was running low.

Hurriedly we finished refueling, took on supplies, and raced back out to reinforce our troops. As we approached their position, I could see they were being overrun. We landed a few feet from where they were engaged in an intense battle. There was no time to extract them, as we were now coming under heavy fire as well. Neither were our soldiers willing to leave. They wanted to finish off what the enemy had started.

We dropped off our supplies of ammunition and water and took off again. With a sense of urgency we rushed back to the base camp for more supplies and to request artillery fire and gunship support for this besieged unit. As we reached our cruising altitude of 3000 feet, we were halfway back to camp just over the Michelin Rubber Plantation.

Suddenly our engine quit.

Immediately we went into emergency procedures in an effort to restart the turbine engine. We worked feverishly but we were falling out of the sky like a rock. I turned on the landing light in preparation for a crash landing. I could see the tops of the trees through the chin bubble at my feet. They were racing up toward us at lightning speed. I paused and thought to myself that in the next few seconds we were all going to die.

As a young boy growing up in church, I had been taught that if you ever found yourself in a place of approaching death, you needed to pray a prayer of contrition to receive pardon for any unsettled business between yourself and God. As I sat in my seat waiting to crash into the trees below, I had no thought of my relationship to God as I really didn't have one.

But God was obviously thinking of me.

Instinctively I turned the radio frequency to the emergency channel and screamed out the universal distress call of "Mayday! Mayday! Mayday! This is Little Bear 21 going down over the Michelin Rubber Plantation!" All of this transpired in just a few seconds. There was little time to think.

Moments before impact where we would literally crash and burn, unexplainably the power came roaring back into our engine. It was as if God had stretched out His hand and caught us. Our helicopter came to a hover just a few feet above the treetops. We then limped back to our base camp alive with our disabled helicopter.

We tried to explain to our superior officers what had happened, but they wouldn't believe us. They said there was no mechanical reason for what we had experienced. The engine and rotor blades were pushed beyond all limits and the aircraft was basically shot. They ended up attributing the whole incident to "pilot error."

Years later, I shared this story with Kathy in the peace and safety of our family room. To our amazement, we realized that at the same time I was going down that night in Vietnam, she was working as a nurse in a hospital in our hometown, thousands of miles and 12 time zones away. She was caring for an elderly nun who was dying of cancer. The sister asked Kathy if there was a special man in her life. Kathy told her that there was this boy she loved who was flying helicopters in Vietnam. Kathy and this dear lady prayed for me that God would watch over and protect me.

That day the sister died, and that night my life was spared.

I don't understand all the mystery involved with the sovereign rule of God and the free will of man where an all-powerful, all loving God allows evil in a world where good things happen to bad people, and bad things happen to good people. Neither can I fathom the incredible honor, privilege and responsibility that God grants His people in prayer. Most of all, I have no answer as to why my life was spared while the lives of thousands of other men were not.

But I do know this: God calls His people to pray and His hand is moved when we do so. And victory in spiritual battle hangs in the balance with the prayers of the saints.

James 5:16b says, "The effective prayer of a righteous man can accomplish much." The context of that promise is healing, but the implications are even broader. If the prayers of righteous people accomplish great things for the kingdom of God, what happens (or doesn't happen!) when the saints do not pray?

Is it possible that a saint struggling with tormenting thoughts of worthlessness or suicidal ideation or panic attacks or other spiritual-mental conflict is enduring needless pain in part because of a lack of prayer, both on the part of the sufferer as well as the body of Christ? In that same chapter, James also says: "Is anyone among you suffering? Then he must pray." (James 5:13a)

In this verse, the primary onus of responsibility for prayer is placed squarely on the shoulders of the one who is suffering. This is a critical point for it is easy for one who is under spiritual attack to feel like a helpless victim. In Christ, that is simply not the case. We may be called to endure suffering, but we still "overwhelmingly conquer through Him who loved us" (Romans 8:37). There are responsibilities that the one who is being attacked must bear; to pray, to confess any and all sin, to renounce lies, to forgive all offenses, to resist the enemy in the authority of Christ.

But the fact remains that when we face times of intense spiritual conflict, our prayers alone may not be enough. We need the army of God to come to our aid through intercession. Even after itemizing the armor of God, the apostle Paul made it clear that we need to be covering one another in prayer. And there are even some Bible teachers who say that one of the main purposes for the armor of God is so we *can* pray! Paul wrote:

> *"With all prayer and petition pray at all times in the Spirit, and with this in view, be on the alert with all perseverance and petition for all the saints, and pray on my behalf, that utterance may be given to me in the opening of my mouth, to make known with boldness the mystery of the gospel..."* (Ephesians 6:18-19).

If the apostle Paul recognized his need for prayer, and called the saints in Ephesus to be on guard, praying with perseverance for him and for each other, then we do well to follow his lead.

Beyond that, the Lord Jesus Himself "would often slip away to the wilderness and pray" (Luke 5:16). And in His hour of most brutal spiritual conflict in the Garden of Gethsemane He took Peter, James and John with Him and asked that they keep watch in prayer along with Him (Mark 13:33-38).

Just in case your experience with prayer has left you with an insipid, bland taste in your mouth, let the words of J. Oswald Sanders in his book, *Spiritual Leadership*, (p.106) stir your heart:

> *"Both our Lord and His bond slave Paul made it clear that true prayer is not pleasant, dreamy reverie. 'All vital praying makes a drain on a man's vitality. True intercession is a sacrifice, a bleeding sacrifice,' wrote J.H. Jowett. Jesus performed many mighty works without outward sign of strain, but of His praying it is recorded, 'He offered up prayers and supplications with strong crying and tears'* (Hebrews 5:7).
>
> *How pale a reflection of Paul and Epaphras' striving and wrestlings are our pallid and languid intercession! 'Epaphras... laboring earnestly for you in his prayers,' wrote Paul to the believers*

at Colossae (Colossians 4:12). And to the same group, 'I wrote that ye knew how great a conflict I have for you' (2:1 KJV). The word for wrestling or conflict, is that from which our 'agonize' is derived. It is used of a man toiling in his work until utterly weary (Colossians 1:29) or competing in the arena for the coveted prize (1 Corinthians 9:25). It describes the soldier battling for his life (1 Timothy 6:12) or a man struggling to deliver his friend from danger (John 18:36). From those and other considerations it is clear that true praying is a strenuous spiritual exercise that demands the utmost mental discipline and concentration."

Years ago, Evelyn Christiansen wrote the book, **What Happens When Women Pray**. It was an important book because in many ways the prayers of godly women have kept the church on its feet and in the battle for a long time. Without a doubt, the entire body of Christ owes an enormous debt to the intercessory prayer ministry of women. I sure do!

But there is a fresh movement in the Spirit. Men are beginning to take leadership and stewardship of this vital ministry of prayer. The old idea that prayer is "soft work" best suited for women, children and the elderly is finally beginning to die. In fact, every church ought to hold a funeral for that lie from the pit of hell! It would be a strong affirmation of the virile ministry of intercessory prayer if every pastor gathered the leaders of his congregation together and prayed for them to be anointed intercessors for the kingdom. And then all those leaders in turn laid hands on the men of the church, crying for God to anoint them in that role as well.

What victories would be won in lives! What battles fought and won for marriages and families! What life, vitality, energy and fruitful, anointed preaching and service would be unleashed for the kingdom!

Too often, I feel that Christian men are spiritually intimidated by their wives and other women in the church. And so our response as men has been to gravitate toward arenas in which we feel more competent, more safe and more secure – in the world of working with our hands and minds rather than with our hearts. Both are needed, but the greater need is for spiritual leaders waging war on their knees.

It would be unthinkable for the U.S. Army to replace the men on the front lines of military combat with women. Should it not be equally unthinkable to, by default, leave the ministry of intercessory prayer to women? Don't get me wrong. I'm not saying women shouldn't pray. God forbid! We need the prayers of women now more than ever! What I am calling for, however, is that men shed this unbiblical notion that the responsibility for holding up the prayer banner in the church and in the home falls mainly on our sisters in Christ.

Have we forgotten that prayer *is* warfare? Timothy Warner reminds us in his book **Spiritual Warfare** (p.134) that:

> *"Prayer is not rear-echelon activity; prayer is front lines spiritual warfare. It*

is the ultimate weapon in our 'struggle... against the rulers, against the authorities, against the powers of this dark world and against the spiritual forces of evil in the heavenly realms' (Ephesians 6:12). It is as S.D. Gordon says in Quiet Talks on Prayer: 'Prayer is striking the winning blow at the concealed enemy. Service is gathering up the results of that blow among the people we see and touch.' In a sense it would be correct to say that prayer is not simply a weapon we use; it is the battle. That is why persevering in prayer is so difficult for most of us."

To pray that God's kingdom come and His will be done on earth as it is in heaven (Matthew 6:10) is an open declaration of war. When we pray in this way, we are asking for God's plans to be accomplished and for the defeat of all demonic schemes, designs and strategies raised up against His plans. Prayer is a direct assault on the enemy of our souls, seeking to rescue spiritual P.O.W.'s, bring home those A.W.O.L. and provide vigorous "air cover" for troops engaged in battle.

I think all of us periodically need a fresh touch from the Lord in the area of prayer. Kathy and I pray for each other, our children, their spouses, our first granddaughter, other friends and family members, the salvation of our non-Christian friends, and the extension of God's Kingdom every day.

If the Lord is showing you that you need to kick up your prayer life a notch or two, trust that He will empower you to do it. But you have to step out in faith and begin even if it feels awkward at first.

With perseverance and prayerful patience and grateful encouragement from our spouses and friends, we can all grow strong in spirit and step up to the plate in prayer leadership. And we have the assurance from God's word that, "in the same way the Spirit helps our weakness, for we do not know how to pray as we should, but the Spirit Himself intercedes for us with groaning's too deep for words; and He who searches the hearts knows what the mind of the Spirit is, because He intercedes for the saints according to the will of God" (Romans 8:26-27).

Only God can make a prayer warrior. He is looking for a few good men... and women. Come on and enlist today!

Dear heavenly Father, You say in Your word that we are to rejoice always, pray without ceasing and to give thanks in everything (1 Thessalonians 5:16-18). And you tell us to be devoted to prayer, keeping alert in it with an attitude of thanksgiving (Colossians 4:2). I can't honestly say that I have done that as consistently as You desire. Thank You for forgiving me for the times I have neglected prayer and tried to live life or wage spiritual battle in my own strength or with my own human resources. I now ask You to rekindle a fire of passion for You and for prayer in my heart. Open my eyes to the spiritual battles in and around me and teach me to wage war on my knees. Thank You for sending the Holy Spirit to be my mentor in prayer. I choose now to shed the old garments of worry, fretting, arguing, controlling and leaning on my own understanding to solve problems. Instead I put on my new garments as a warrior in prayer. In Jesus' name I ask these things, Amen.

Chapter Seven

Under Cover

The U.S. military base at Cu Chi was built on land that was flat and dry, in an area that had been primarily used for cattle and vegetable farming.

Directly northeast of our base camp were the deadly Ho Bo Woods, and the infamous Iron Triangle. These were favorite hiding places for the enemy, and staging grounds for assaults against Saigon. They were filled with tunnel and bunker complexes lined with booby traps and storage areas for the enemy. Not far to the north was a triple canopy jungle which many believed was the command center for all Viet Cong operations. To the south, the tranquil Oriental River flowed, serving as a supply line between VC bases.

Despite its strategic and precarious position, it never ceased to amaze me how much safer I felt returning to base camp after any mission I flew. It was the closest thing to home I had during my tour of duty in the Vietnam War. Once I crossed the perimeter into the camp, parked my helicopter in its bunker and shut the engine down, I thought everything would be all right. But many nights we would receive incoming rocket and mortar fire from outside the perimeter.

Once the first rounds began to impact the barracks, the flight line where our aircraft were parked, and the fuel and ammunition depots, sirens would go off and we'd run to the bunkers just outside our "hootches."

"Hootch" was a term of endearment for the makeshift barracks where we slept. They were surrounded by sandbags designed to keep shrapnel from these incoming rounds from wounding or killing us. Despite these efforts at safeguarding us from harm, the barracks were not sufficient to withstand direct hits. On the other hand, the underground bunkers outside our barracks could withstand almost anything the enemy might throw at us.

For the child of God, safety and security is not found in the buildings where we worship or even in the houses in which we dwell. As a matter of fact, these places often are the primary targets and foci of the enemy's attacks. The only true sanctuary for the child of God is in Christ, living life under cover... His cover.

King David was more skilled and experienced in battle than most of us ever will be or ever care to be. In the following verses from Psalm 18, it is evident where His security lay:

> *"I love You, O LORD, my strength. The LORD is my rock and my fortress and my deliverer, my God, my rock, in whom I take refuge; my shield and the horn of my salvation, my stronghold. I call upon*

the LORD, who is worthy to be praised, and I am saved from my enemies... The LORD my God illumines my darkness. For by You I can run upon a troop; and by my God I can leap over a wall. As for God, His way is blameless; the word of the LORD is tried; He is a shield to all who take refuge in Him, for who is God, but the LORD? And who is a rock, except our God..." (Psalm 18:1-3, 28-31).

This sentiment is vividly captured again in Psalm 91 that reminds us that we are secure in God:

"He who dwells in the shelter of the Most High will abide in the shadow of the Almighty. I will say to the LORD, 'My refuge and my fortress, my God, in whom I trust!' For it is He who delivers you from the snare of the trapper and from the deadly pestilence. He will cover you with His pinions, and under His wings you may seek refuge; His faithfulness is a shield and bulwark. You will not be afraid of the terror by night, or of the arrow that flies by day." (Psalm 91:1-5).

We need to realize that the whole strategy of waging and winning spiritual battle in the kingdom of God rises or falls on the question of *authority*. And the privilege of exercising spiritual authority is only granted to those who operate *under* spiritual authority.

Those in the military naturally understand this concept of authority better than civilians. And even though I did not grasp the principles of spiritual warfare illustrated during our missions in Vietnam at the time, I can see them now.

For example, though I was well-trained to fly and experienced in flying helicopters, I never took off on my own. I was always involved in a mission that was designed and coordinated by those higher up the chain of command. Pilots like myself were given orders by our commanding officers. In spiritual battle, God Himself designs the warfare strategies and assigns us our missions. We learn to listen and submit to His authority in dependent prayer.

When we were flying, often times we couldn't see where we were going and so we had to rely on the tower operator, Cu Chi radar and other radio communications coming in. It would have been foolish and potentially deadly for us to refuse their guidance. Likewise, when we launch out by faith into a mission the Lord calls us to accomplish, we don't always know what to do. We may think we do, but we really don't. We are operating in unknown territory and so the Lord has provided His Holy Spirit to lead us. In fact, that is a promise in Scripture which says, "For all who are being led by the Spirit of God, these are sons of God" (Romans 8:14).

The missions we flew were successful only to the degree that we obeyed our leaders and did our jobs in accordance with the training we'd received. That's how the military has always operated. And that is the way things work in the spiritual world as well.

In Luke 7, the story is told of a centurion (a soldier in charge of 100 men) in the town of Capernaum who had a very sick slave. This centurion, though a Roman, was highly respected by the Jews and loved the nation of Israel. He had even built the local synagogue (vv. 1-5).

As Jesus headed toward the soldier's house, friends of the centurion intercepted Him and gave Jesus a message. We'll pick up Luke's account from there:

> *"Lord, do not trouble Yourself further, for I am not worthy for You to come under my roof; for this reason I did not even consider myself worthy to come to You, but just say the word, and my servant will be healed. For I also am a man placed under authority, with soldiers under me; and I say to this one, 'Go!' and he goes, and to another, 'Come!' and he comes, and to my slave, 'Do this!' and he does it"* (Luke 7:6b-8).

Jesus was astonished at this Gentile soldier's faith and announced to the crowd, "I say to you, not even in Israel have I found such great faith" (Luke 7:9).

What was it about this man's faith that caused Jesus to marvel so much? Certainly a large part of it was that the soldier recognized in Jesus the capacity to heal from far away as well as he could in person. But there is another component to it. The centurion recognized that Jesus, like himself, was "also a man placed under authority." Not a man *with* authority (though Jesus was certainly that!), but a man *under* authority.

In John 5:19 (and John 15:30 and elsewhere), Jesus stated categorically that He operated totally under the authority of God the Father. John wrote:

> ***"Therefore Jesus answered and was saying to them, 'Truly, truly, I say to you, the Son can do nothing of Himself unless it is something He sees the Father doing; for whatever the Father does, these things the Son also does in like manner.'***

Each of the devil's temptations of Jesus, during His 40 days of fasting in the wilderness, was an attempt to get Jesus to act apart from submission to the Father's authority. The devil urged Jesus to zap a rock and turn it into a loaf of bread. He then encouraged Him to take His own path to authority over the nations and become king the fast and easy way by worshipping the devil. And finally, Satan encouraged Him to wow the crowds by taking a flying leap off the temple, thus demanding that God would provide a huge angelic cushion to break His fall (see Luke 4:1-13).

But Jesus would have none of it. He didn't enter into discussion. He didn't try to match wits with the devil. He didn't try to beat Him in an argument. Jesus, filled with the Holy Spirit, stood under the authority of the Father and three times quoted the authoritative Word of God. And the devil took off.

Why do you think that Jesus, the Son of God and God Himself, chose to live life on earth without one shred of self-reliance? He was showing us the way we are to live in respect to our heavenly Father.

Where do you stand today in relation to the authority of God in your life? Where does your heart stand in regard to the human authorities He has placed over you? Knowing how easy it is to let this matter of submission "slide," please, for the sake of your own life, family and church prayerfully look over the following Scriptures:

> *"But He gives a greater grace. Therefore it says, 'God is opposed to the proud, but gives grace to the humble.' Submit therefore to God. Resist the devil and he will flee from you."* (James 4:6,7)

> *"You younger men, likewise, be subject to your elders; and all of you, clothe yourselves with humility toward one another, for God is opposed to the proud, but gives grace to the humble. Therefore humble yourselves under the mighty hand of God, that He may exalt you at the proper time." (1 Peter 5:5,6)*

> *"Honor your father and mother which is the first commandment with a promise, so that it may be well with you, and that you may live long on the earth." (Ephesians 6:2,3)*

> *"Wives, be subject to your own husbands, as to the Lord. For the husband is the head of the wife, as Christ also is the head of the church, He Himself being*

the Savior of the body. But as the church is subject to Christ, also the wives ought to be to their husbands in everything. Husbands, love your wives, just as Christ also loved the church and gave Himself up for her..." (Ephesians 5:22-25).

"Every person is to be in subjection to the governing authorities. For there is no authority except from God, and those which exist are established by God. Therefore whoever resists authority has opposed the ordinance of God; and they who have opposed will receive condemnation upon themselves... Therefore it is necessary to be in subjection, not only because of wrath, but also for conscience' sake. For because of this you also pay taxes, for rulers are servants of God, devoting themselves to this very thing. Render to all what is due them; tax to whom tax is due; custom to whom custom; fear to whom fear; honor to whom honor." (Romans 13:1,2,5-7)

"Act as free men, and do not use your freedom as a covering for evil, but use it as bond slaves of God. Honor all people, love the brotherhood, fear God, honor the king. Servants, be submissive to your masters with all respect, not only

to those who are good and gentle, but also to those who are unreasonable. For this finds favor, if for the sake of conscience toward God a person bears up under sorrows when suffering unjustly."
(1 Peter 2:16-19)

"Slaves, in all things obey those who are your masters on earth, not with external service, as those who merely please men, but with sincerity of heart, fearing the Lord. Whatever you do, do your work heartily, as for the Lord rather than for men, knowing that from the Lord you will receive the reward of the inheritance. It is the Lord Christ whom you serve. For he who does wrong will receive the consequences of the wrong which he has done, and that without partiality." (Colossians 3:22-25)

"Obey your leaders and submit to them, for they keep watch over your souls as those who will give an account. Let them do this with joy and not with grief, for this would be unprofitable for you." (Hebrews 13:17)

You may feel a bit bombarded by all these Scriptures. We did that for a reason. This mentality of self-sufficiency, self-reliance, self-determination, self-promotion and selfish ambition is so rampant in our national psyche (and tragically, in the church as well) that we felt like we needed to launch a bit of a Scriptural artillery barrage.

If you have been living life on the ragged edge of independence and isolation, we earnestly call you to come under the protective care of God and the authorities that He has placed over you. That is the only place of spiritual safety available to you.

If you have already been living in humility and submission, we commend you and encourage you to continue to walk in this way. By so doing you are well on your way to winning the spiritual battles in your life.

Please understand what we are saying, however. Submission does not mean being a door mat. It does not mean being afraid to state your opinion or express your disagreement to an authority figure. It is an attitude of trust and dependence upon God Himself. And it is believing that He will work in and through those imperfect authorities in your life; in your home, in the marketplace, in the church and in the community. And that attitude of trust and dependence results in respectfully expressing oneself while humbly submitting and obeying, even if what we are being asked to do is not our preference.

In those instances when human authorities abuse the power that they have, it is right and just for those under authority to seek help from a higher authority. A verbally abusive coach should be reported to the athletic director. A Sunday School teacher who is teaching error should be reported to the Sunday School superintendent. A man who is physically or sexually abusing his wife and kids should be reported to local authorities. A pastor who misuses his authority over the congregation should be held accountable by church or denominational leadership. A police officer who brutally beats a suspect must be held accountable by a court of law. A Congressman who refuses to act in accordance with the populace he represents should be voted out of office. And so on.

In those moments when human authorities fail at the highest level to do what is right and instead seek to force us to do what is wrong or not do what is right, then we must obey God rather than men (see Acts 4:18-20).

In the realm of spiritual warfare, the matter of submission becomes an issue of cosmic consequences. James 4:7 says, "Submit therefore to God. Resist the devil and he will flee from you." What is going to happen if you don't first submit to God's authority, including the human authorities over you? What will happen if you try to resist the devil when you are not under that protective authority-shield? He will certainly not flee and in fact, may turn and cause serious damage to you and your loved ones.

John Paul Jackson, in his book *Needless Casualties of War*, (p. 44) warns against believers engaging in presumptuous spiritual battle. By this he means individuals or groups of people verbally confronting high level powers of darkness without a calling from God and a clear covering of protection from the church. This sort of activity can be born of impatience or pride. Spiritual "loose cannons" (those operating in a self-proclaimed "apostolic" or "prophetic" manner, but refusing to come under wise, healthy, balanced spiritual authority) present a grave danger to themselves and others. Jackson's use of war movies to illustrate spiritual truth provides a wise admonition:

"In the movie, Navy Seals, there was a young naval officer who was ordered by his commanding officer to carry out a stealth infiltration/exfiltration operation. Although the officer was gifted, he constantly endangered missions by taking unnecessary gambles. On one mission everything was going like clockwork until the young officer ran out from under cover and fired on the enemy, although he had prior orders not to do so. Consequently, he endangered the mission and the people around him. As a result, a team member died in a deadly firefight. A similar loss of judgment is illustrated in the movie, Saving Private Ryan. Tom Hanks plays a Ranger infantry captain who is ordered to find Private Ryan and escort him to safety. In one scene, Hanks' character has a tragic loss of judgment. His judgment is clouded not because of thrill-seeking or ego gratification but because of battle fatigue. He orders his unit into an unnecessary skirmish that has little to do with his mission. They succeed, but at a great cost. They lost valuable team members."

It is easy to get intoxicated with the notion that we are on the winning side and begin to view ourselves as spiritual S.W.A.T. team members that are invincible in whatever we set our minds to do. Jesus warned against such potentially disastrous spiritual giddiness when He told His disciples:

> *"Behold, I have given you authority to tread on serpents and scorpions, and over all the power of the enemy, and nothing will injure you. Nevertheless do not rejoice in this, that the demons are subject to you, but rejoice that your names are recorded in heaven."* (Luke 10:19-20).

As the disciples went out to preach the gospel and heal the sick, they were confronted by the powers of darkness, and so will we. In the midst of their ministry to hurting and needy people, they dispatched the demons that were harassing those people, and so can we. Where believers in Christ have suffered harm, however, is in venturing into realms of spiritual battle where even angels would fear to tread. For example, a believer in Christ from America does not have spiritual authority to travel to China and demand that the gods of Chinese communism release their hold on that nation. Rather than futilely trying to exercise authority we don't have anyway, why not obey the Scriptures and follow God's battle plan for transformation:

> *"First of all, then, I urge that entreaties and prayers, petitions and thanksgivings, be made on behalf of all men, for kings and all who are in authority, so*

that we may lead a tranquil and quiet life in all godliness and dignity. This is good and acceptable in the sight of God our Savior, who desires all men to be saved and to come to the knowledge of the truth... Therefore I want the men in every place to pray, lifting up holy hands, without wrath and dissension" (1 Timothy 2:1-4,8).

That's a battle plan for spiritual warfare, a mighty weapon of mass destruction to the domain of darkness and a mighty weapon of mass reconstruction of the kingdom of God that will give glory to Him not men. And which will spare us from many needless casualties of war. It will come when God's people are walking in freedom, as Isaiah predicted:

"The Spirit of the Lord GOD is upon me, because the LORD has anointed me to bring good news to the afflicted; He has sent me to bind up the brokenhearted, to proclaim liberty to captives and freedom to prisoners; to proclaim the favorable year of the LORD and the day of vengeance of our God; to comfort all who mourn, to grant those who mourn in Zion, giving them a garland instead of ashes, the oil of gladness instead of mourning, the mantle of praise instead of a spirit of fainting. So they will be called oaks of righteousness,

the planting of the LORD, that He may be glorified. Then they will rebuild the ancient ruins, they will raise up the former devastations; and they will repair the ruined cities, the desolations of many generations" (Isaiah 61:1-4).

Dear heavenly Father, I recognize that humility and submission to authority is not only Your will, and therefore good, acceptable and perfect, but it is the way Jesus Himself walked. Please forgive me for the times I have foolishly believed I could do whatever I felt was right and that somehow I would be protected. Forbid it, Lord, that I should ever put You to the test again. I now run into the strong tower that is Your name and know that, in seeking to walk in humility, submission and dependence on You, I will be safe. I also acknowledge that I desperately need the body of Christ. Knit my heart together with other believers so that corporately we can discern Your mind and accomplish Your purposes. In the gentle and humble name of Jesus I pray, Amen.

Chapter Eight

Dirty Tricks

If you were the enemy, what would you do to take out the forces opposed to you? Wouldn't you hit them at their weakest, most vulnerable point? Wouldn't you try to avoid detection, sneak past their defenses, create confusion and strike from within their own perimeter at the place where they least expected it?

In Vietnam, even though our enemy was massively overmatched by American firepower, the North Vietnamese Army (NVA) and Viet Cong (VC) were masters at guerilla warfare, and used every trick and strategy at their disposal. Our soldiers were trained in conventional warfare and fighting an enemy we could not see was frustrating at best and deadly at worst.

Often we would need to seek cover from our barracks into bunkers when incoming mortar and rocket fire hit our base camp most every night. When I arrived at Cu Chi in September, 1969 I had a very rude awakening on my third night there. What happened that night with all the explosions was scary enough. The reason for those night attacks and many others like it, still sends chills up my spine to this day. I still duck when I hear a car back fire.

I was trying to get some sleep in the hot, mosquito, cockroach and rat infested hootch to which I had been assigned to with the other pilots from my unit. I soon fell into a very deep sleep. I hadn't had much sleep since leaving the States and getting settled into this war zone, and I was dog tired.

Suddenly I woke up to the sounds of explosions going off all around me and shrapnel coming through the walls. The barracks were surrounded by sand bags piled only high enough to prevent the shrapnel from penetrating the thin, screened-in walls built around our cots. But as I sat up, I was sprayed with dirt and sand coming through the screens above my head. Looking around, I saw that everyone else in this makeshift shelter had already vacated the premises for the underground bunkers outside.

Having never experienced incoming rocket and mortar fire before, I was disoriented and didn't know what to do. I felt like a fool being the last one to stumble into the heavily fortified bunker out back. The rest of the pilots were already sitting around this damp, dingy hole in the ground in their OD green underwear, unstrapped combat helmets hanging around their heads, drinking beer. They laughed heartily as they watched the "new guy" barely escaping death come tumbling onto the dirt floor with a look of fear in his eyes.

I understood right then and there that I could never afford to sleep that deeply again. From that night on, and for many years after, I never would.

I soon found out that this was a typical night at Cu Chi. On many nights we could receive upwards of 60-70 rounds of incoming fire. The NVA and VC were using one of their favorite tactics against large military installations such as ours. Their purpose was to steal our sense of safety and security, kill us and destroy our military assets. They wanted us to know that they could attack us any time they desired, thus forcing us to use our sizeable resources in defending the base camp rather than in launching assaults against them. The result was a serious deterioration of morale because we felt helpless to defend ourselves. We never knew, day or night, when these enemy missiles might come slamming down on top of us or around us. It was never safe to let your guard down.

Why was the enemy able to launch such consistent, devastating attacks on us inside the barbed wired fortress of Cu Chi that was then the size of a small city in the U.S. ? Most soldiers thought that it was because of VC informers who came in from surrounding villages and worked at the base camp. But that was not the main reason.

An account of a 1966 operation designed to discover the military and political headquarters of the VC's 4th Military region (just north of Cu Chi) shows that the mystery surrounding our area had been baffling the U.S. Army for years. Robert Martin in his book, *The Tunnel Rats* (p.1) wrote:

> *"As the operation progressed, the Americans came under VC sniper fire and engaged in small firefights. However, as our soldiers approached the areas where their adversaries apparently were, there was no trace of them. The days progressed and the American*

> *casualties began to mount, but the frustrated soldiers were unable to engage the enemy and could only find some foxholes, trenches, and large caches of rice. Little did they know that the Vietcong were always only a few yards away."*

The reason this military operation failed to effectively engage the enemy was the same reason our base camp at Cu Chi came under such elusive attacks. No one knew it at the time, but our base camp at Cu Chi had been built over an elaborate tunnel system constructed in the 1940's during Vietnam's war with France. This tunnel complex had been expanded considerably in the 1960's so that it stretched 130 miles or more from the border of Cambodia to Saigon. It provided the enemy with a totally secretive means of moving thousands of troops and supplies into position to advance or retreat. And it provided the perfect cover for small bands of saboteurs, as the following account from Tim Page & John Pimlott writing in the book, *Nam: The Vietnam Experience* (p.43) described the situation in the following commentary:

> *"When the American 25th Infantry Division first arrived in 1966, an enterprising Viet Cong called Huynh Van Co hid with two comrades underneath the [Cu Chi] camp for a week, emerging at night to wreak havoc and steal food. The newly arrived 25th were baffled by the attacks, assuming that mortar fire was coming in from outside their perimeter.*

> *But, in the words of one general, they had bivouac'd on a volcano. After causing psychological damage out of all proportion to its military importance, Huynh Van Co and the others withdrew to the "belt" of tunnels surrounding the base. Neither they nor their tunnels were ever detected."*

This often three-tiered underground network of tunnels spanned from the surface down to 30 or more feet deep. It included wells, airshafts, war rooms, mess halls, infirmaries, sleeping quarters, storage depots as well as staging points from which to attack. Remarkably, even training sites were located in the brutally hot, humid and disease-infested environment under the earth. The ground consisted mainly of clay, and when dry, this reddish-brown Laterite became hard as rock – perfect tunneling material.

The entrances to these tunnels were extremely well-hidden and often very well-guarded. Any of our unwary soldiers could step into punji pits with bamboo spikes smeared with dung. These poisoned stakes pierced the boot and foot, causing painful, debilitating infections. Worse yet was the terrible psychological effect on our troops. Even if a soldier never encountered a punji pit, the mere thought that he might was enough to make him hesitate at each step. Often booby traps of explosives were set around the entrances so that anyone attempting to follow the enemy would be maimed or killed.

Inside the tunnels, other explosive booby traps were set as were trip wires that would release scorpions or poisonous snakes. Purposely constructed with various dips and turns ranging from 60-120 degrees. Our soldiers never knew what waited for them around the next bend. Sometimes the Vietcong would wait in a dark chamber for an unsuspecting American soldier to enter. Then, once the soldier peered into the aperture, the VC would garrote him or slit his throat.

Although most of us would not have been caught dead in one of these tunnels, a very special breed of soldier (both South Vietnamese and American) was born to fight an underground war to root out the enemy. These men came to be known as "tunnel rats." Armed with only a flashlight, handgun and knife, these extraordinary brave men became an elite group in Vietnam. Captain Herbert Thornton, the "father of the tunnel rats," commented on the unusual courage and temperament required to fight such a war in the book, ***NAM: The Vietnamese Experience*** (p. 43-44):

> *"It took a special kind of being. He had to have an inquisitive mind, a lot of guts, and a lot of real moxie into knowing what to touch and what not to touch to stay alive because you could blow yourself out of there in a heartbeat."*

But one did not have to go underground to be in danger of booby traps. Trip wires set up along trails, in underwater places where soldiers must cross, and in seemingly innocuous places in villages that could maim or kill without warning. The trauma and stress on battle-weary, shell-shocked soldiers was incalculable.

In addition to the approximately 58,000 U.S. soldiers killed, over 300,000 Americans were injured in this military conflict with a largely invisible enemy. Our forces inflicted heavy damage on the enemy as well with our B-52 bombers being an especially potent weapon. But in retrospect, our ignorance of the enemy's tactics of guerilla warfare resulted in far more American casualties than would have been the case had we understood his strategy from the beginning.

The same thing is true of spiritual warfare.

We often get calls for help from individuals, couples and families who have or are experiencing the fallout from adultery, pornography, drug and alcohol addictions, childhood sexual abuse, eating disorders, people cutting on themselves and any number of dysfunctional ways that people try to cope with trauma. The litany of suffering and torment from personal sin and victimization can go on and on. PTSD (post-traumatic stress disorder) is not unique to just military trauma, but to anyone who has been hurt or abused in any situation apart from combat trauma.

Four couples at a recent marriage conference confessed that their attendance at that event was their last hope for a marriage torn apart by adultery.

The question often asked us is, "Are these spiritual, psychological or physiological problems?" The answer is that they are often all of the above.

Our problems always involve the spiritual area of our lives, because every struggle affects our relationship with God. Plus the possibility of being tempted, accused, deceived, threatened and even physically attacked by the powers of darkness is an ever-present reality. And it is certainly never safe to take off the armor of God.

In addition our problems are always psychological, for they affect our mind (what we believe), our emotions (how we feel), and our will (the decisions we make). Finally, spiritual and psychological problems can result in physical health issues and vice versa.

This is not to say that the complexity of human bondage is not at times maddening, and the resolution of such entrapment can seem next to impossible. We can feel as confused and frustrated as those soldiers trying to engage an enemy they could not see. Though a complete analysis of all the whys and wherefores of sin and suffering is well beyond the scope of this book, in the rest of this chapter we desire to shine more light into the dark tunnel network of our spiritual enemies.

The Bible teaches that we are up against three primary enemies: the world, the flesh and the devil.

The **world** (translated from the Greek *kosmos*) refers to cultural philosophies, peer pressures, practices and paraphernalia of people who are opposed to God. 1 John 2:15-17 warns:

> *"Do not love the world nor the things in the world. If anyone loves the world, the love of the Father is not in him. For all that is in the world, the lust of the flesh and the lust of the eyes and the boastful pride of life, is not from the Father, but is from the world. The world is passing away, and also its lusts; but the one who does the will of God lives forever."*

Things in this world appeal to the lust of the flesh (our human appetites out of control) and the lust of the eyes (our consuming desire to possess what is beautiful) and the boastful pride of life (the selfish passion to appear successful, smart, powerful, wealthy, religious etc.). None of these things is part of God's good provision for us.

The **flesh** is that part of us which was well-trained early in life to operate in self-sufficiency rather than God-dependency. It carries over into adulthood and acts in opposition to God's Spirit, as the apostle Paul described in Galatians 5:16-17:

> *"But I say, walk by the Spirit, and you will not carry out the desire of the flesh. For the flesh sets its desire against the Spirit, and the Spirit against the flesh; for these are in opposition to one another, so that you may not do the things that you please."*

Fleshly deeds include sexual sins of the mind and body, spiritual sins of worshiping false gods, witchcraft, drug and alcohol addictions, raucous parties, strife and quarrels, jealousy and envy, angry outbursts and other things like these (see Galatians 5:22-23).

The **devil** controls the world system (1 John 5:19) and tries to entice us to love the things of the world rather than Christ. One of his names is "tempter" (e.g. Matthew 4:3). He will aggressively use the things we see, hear, taste, touch and smell in order to seek to lure us into sin. In addition, sometimes "out of the blue" he will plant a tempting thought in our minds. For example, a critical judgment of a person's motives to see if we'll take the bait and go down his road. The bottom line is that Satan and his demons are exploiters of the flaws in our character, weaknesses in our will and chinks in our spiritual armor. He is especially ruthless in his attack when he detects that we are seeking to get our needs for acceptance, security and significance met outside of who we are in Christ.

However, the flesh can also be the source of temptation in these areas without the devil's help. The flesh tries to get us to milk attention, pleasure and approval from the world around us rather than seeking God and His provision. James wrote:

> ***"Let no one say when he is tempted, "I am being tempted by God; for God cannot be tempted by evil, and He Himself does not tempt anyone. But each one is tempted when he is carried away and enticed by his own lust. Then when lust has conceived, it gives birth to sin; and when sin is accomplished, it brings forth death. Do not be deceived, my beloved brethren"*** (James 1:13-16).

So how might these three enemies attempt to triple-team us and trap us? Using legal language, **the flesh** provides the *means,* our tendency to live our lives independently from God, **the devil**, acting as tempter and deceiver, provides the *motive* (by lying to us and making us think sin is a good thing), and **the world** provides the *opportunity* (through the people, places, and things around us that are in opposition to God and His will). Neil Anderson and Tim Warner help us understand this three-pronged assault in their book, ***Beginner's Guide to Spiritual Warfare*** (p.44):

> *"Discussions of spiritual warfare sooner or later get around to asking what the relationship is between the world, the flesh and the devil. Paul introduces all three elements into his definitive statement about this warfare in Ephesians 2:1-3. Notice the way he links the world, the flesh and the devil together. He does not suggest that sometimes it is the world we are dealing with, sometimes, the flesh, and sometimes the devil. Paul sees them working so closely together that you really can't understand one without seeing the way it relates to the others."*

They conclude their exegesis of this passage by saying (p.50):

> *"So, in talking about the world, the flesh, and the devil, we need to understand that it is not all one or all the other. Most of the time it is not even mostly one or the other. They work together, and we need a strategy for resistance that takes into account all three without allowing an emphasis on one of them to dominate."*

The questions that cry out for answers are: Is this battle for the mind a winnable war? Is it truly possible for those caught in sin's chains and the devil's dirtiest tricks to escape into the freedom Christ purchased at Calvary? Can temptation be overcome? Can addictions be broken? Can the voice of the accuser be silenced? Can deceit and denial be exposed and truth embraced from the heart?

The devil lurks and works in the darkness of shame, seclusion and denial, seeking to lure us deeper and deeper into bondage. God is light and operates in the brightness of truth, honesty and genuine transparency, seeking to release us into freedom.

We devoted a whole chapter to the importance of prayer, but we simply cannot overstate its importance. Prayer opens doors that no man or power of hell can shut.

As you pray, recognize that sometimes things get worse before they get better. In order for some people to look up they've got to hit rock bottom. As long as they can come up with one more techniques of self-rescue, most people caught in addictions will try to pull themselves up by their own bootstraps.

True freedom from sin's control and true healing from sin's scars must always come in the context of community. Isolation is one of the devil's most effective weapons and that's why the Bible continually reminds us of our responsibility toward one another. Love another (1 John 4:7), encourage one another (Hebrews 3:13), teach and admonish one another (Colossians 3:16) are just a sampling of these Scriptural exhortations to live out our Christian lives in relationship to community.

The devil wants to use guilt, shame and the fear of being judged and condemned to keep people trapped in their secret world of sin. Don't let him. All the talk in the world about the love of God without the assurance of real flesh and blood believers living out that love is worthless. "Little children, let us not love with word or with tongue, but in deed and truth" (1 John 3:18).

"Beloved, if God so loved us, we also ought to love one another. No one has seen God at any time, if we love one another, God abides in us, and His love is perfected in us" (1 John 4:11-12). Of course, this kind of love is only possible through the power of the Holy Spirit.

The weapon of *truth* when brought in behind the "air cover" of prayer and the artillery fire of love can truly be like the rescue helicopters we flew in Vietnam. In the next chapter we'll talk about how to bring truth into an environment of grace in order to set captives free. For now, it is enough to know that Jesus taught:

> *"If you continue in My word, then you are truly disciples of Mine; and you will know the truth, and the truth will make you free... Truly, truly, I say to you, everyone who commits sin is the slave of sin. The slave does not remain in the house forever; the son does remain forever. So if the Son makes you free, you will be free indeed"* (John 8:31-36).

Every sin that controls us is fueled by lies that we have believed. Every dirty trick of the evil one to cause us to rebel against God is sin. There are no exceptions. And once you recognize the lie, reject it as such and embrace the truth, then freedom comes. What I have just described is called repentance, a change of mind that results in a change of life.

When repentance comes, true repentance, then all heaven breaks loose!

> *Dear heavenly Father, all this talk about my enemies is a little unnerving. But I thank You that nowhere in Your word do you instruct me to be afraid of the devil. "Greater is He who is in [me] than he who is in the world." That's what 1 John 4:4 says and I choose to believe it. I refuse to be anxious, but instead I'll "be of sober spirit" and "on the alert." I admit to You, Jesus, that I am not strong enough in myself to resist temptation, silence accusation or sniff out deception. I need You to be My spiritual radar to grant me that kind of discernment. And in the areas where I continue to fall and fail, dear Lord, I cry out to You to rescue me. I thank You that nothing is too difficult for You and I stand against the enemy's attempt to steal hope from me. I trust that freedom is for me, too, even as I continue to take responsibility for choosing truth and getting the help I need. In Jesus who is the way, truth and life I pray, Amen.*

Chapter Nine

Prisoners of War

In 1970 I was part of a very large military force that former President Nixon ordered to invade Cambodia. A 25 mile limit was set as to how far we could go into this "neutral" country in order to take out enemy depots and disrupt supply lines and troop shipments streaming down the Ho Chi Minh trail into South Vietnam. Our forces set up in a makeshift staging area just north of Tay Ninh City near the Cambodian border.

Our helicopter unit flew a number of different missions during this invasion and for the first three days and nights I don't remember sleeping much, if at all. We were in the air most of the time, the action was very intense. Even though the enemy had advanced warning of our invasion, many refused to retreat behind the 25 mile line of demarcation and chose to stay and fight to the death.

One of our missions was to do BDA's (bomb damage assessments) after US Air Force jets had made their bombing raids into the area. The North Vietnamese had a number of SAM (surface to air missile) sites set up to take out our jets. While conducting these missions we would often see a number of our pilots ejecting from their jet aircraft after being hit.

We would always do our best to rescue them before they were captured. Too often we couldn't get to them fast enough and they would be caught by the NVA and taken to prisoner of war camps in North Vietnam.

One cloudy, rainy day in March, 1970, I was flying over a place called the Straight Edge Woods. It was a large, ominous, thick stand of triple canopy forest straddling the Cambodian and Vietnamese borders between Cu Chi and Tay Ninh. We called it "The Enchanted Forest."

Normally I would have avoided this place like the plague. It was a dangerous stronghold of the enemy and we had no "friendlies" near enough to help us if we got into trouble there.

A few weeks earlier flying over this location an RPG (rocket propelled grenade) had exploded just behind my tail rotor, and so I hated and feared flying in this area with a passion. I don't remember how these insidious weapons worked or why it exploded prematurely behind us, I was just thankful it didn't hit my tail rotor.

As I headed south along the edge of the woods just east of the huge, muddy Van Co Dong River, one of our ground units operating near the area saw us flying over their position and contacted us on our radio frequency. They thought they had just spotted a patrol of NVA regular forces marching several captured GI's north through these woods toward the Cambodian border. They were headed to a POW camp in Hanoi.

The message sent chills through my entire crew as they listened over their headsets. Every soldier knew what happened to captured American soldiers. For them, survival during the march was doubtful and death would be welcomed should they make it all the way to the prison camp. There was no way we were going to let this happen to them if we could help it.

I radioed my command center at Cu Chi and told my CO (commanding officer) where we were and our change of flight plans. I did not wait for a response or permission. Immediately I turned my aircraft toward this jungle hell. We quickly dropped to tree top level, 200 ft. above the forest floor, and started searching through the dense foliage for trails and any sign of our friends.

This maneuver put us all in a great danger of enemy fire, but my entire crew was ready to jump out of the helicopter if needed in order to free our fellow soldiers from captivity.

We searched as long as our fuel load would allow and followed the trails we could find through the woods overhead. We spotted what we thought to be a few makeshift camps and/or possible holding stations. We even landed in a few of these spots in the hope of rescuing our men, even though we had no gunship backup.

Over and over again, signs of their presence were there, but they were nowhere in sight. With little fuel left to continue, we were forced to abandon our search. Turning our helicopter around to return to base camp was one of the most disheartening moments in my tour of duty in Nam.

When captured, many of our POW's were sent to the Hoa Lo prison complex in the center of Hanoi, North Vietnam. Our soldiers nicknamed this place "Heartbreak Hotel" and the "Hanoi Hilton." "New Guy Village" was where new POW's were received and "Las Vegas" is where torture sessions were regularly held.

These compounds were small and dirty. Legs were forced into shackles with a pipe and rope to lock them in place. Arms were tied behind your back from above the elbow to the wrists. A foot from a guard placed in your back would tighten the ropes so that they cut into your bones. You wouldn't bleed because these bindings would act like a tourniquet.

You were thrown into a space not much bigger than your body as you lay on a cement slab. No medical care was given and two meals a day of pumpkin or cabbage soup would keep you alive but without the nutrients to ward off disease. Sitting in your own human waste with no ability to ward off the rats and spiders crawling over you was terrifying. And with no windows, the darkness was complete.

No one can be taught to survive such brutality. The cruelty was designed to break your resistance and provide the enemy with a sadistic measure of pleasure as he exerted his power over you. In this kind of bondage, you can only maintain your sanity and hold on for so long.

Every soldier dreaded the possibility of becoming a prisoner of war. Medals of honor were awarded to men who did everything in their power to save their fellow soldiers' lives and prevent them from being taken captive. Most of these awards are bestowed posthumously because someone was willing to lay down his life for a friend. Jesus said there is no greater love than this (John 15:13).

None of us set out to be heroes. We were all just scared young boys, called to be soldiers to do a job for our country. Some of us might have been more committed, resourceful, stubborn or naïve than other soldiers. But every one of us was ready to face what was in the darkness, because we were fighting for one another. Whether we lived or died, we would do it for each other, because in combat that was all we had.

During those days in Vietnam, a seed was planted in my heart that did not begin to grow or bear fruit until after I came to know Jesus Christ as my Savior and Lord. This was the unquenchable yearning to rescue others who were trapped by the enemy. I have since come to understand that perhaps 85% or more of the body of Christ is in varying degrees oppressed and in bondage to the world, flesh and devil. They are spiritual prisoners of war. And by God's enabling grace, they must be set free.

After coming to Christ and spending three years of intense discipleship training and growth at our new local church in Wisconsin, Kathy and I sensed the Lord calling us into full time Christian service. We applied with the Evangelical Free Church Mission and were assigned to Zaire, Africa in 1983 as career missionaries.

Late in 1984 I was attending a pastor's conference in a small rural village in Zaire. I was walking with a group of pastors when we noticed a teenage boy following us. He made his way to the front of our group and stared directly into my eyes. I could tell there was something seriously wrong with him, and his intent toward us appeared to be malevolent. Our group stopped and I asked him in the trade language of Lingala, *"Ozali nani?"* This is literally translated, "Who are you?" but is generally understood as "What is your name?" His response was, *"Tozali mingi"* or "We are many." It was clear that this was the same type of evil presence that I had experienced in my past, but I still had no idea how to respond to it, let alone how to help this young man be set free.

I expected that the native pastors I was with knew what to do. After all, this was their land and people. But they seemed as confused and fearful as I was. After 60 years of missionary presence in Zaire, they had been deeply infected with our western worldview.

Dr. Timothy Warner, veteran missionary, missiologist, my doctoral mentor and good friend wrote in his book, *Spiritual Warfare* (p.130):

> *"One of the more obvious types of power encounter is the casting out of demons. Unfortunately, not many missionaries or evangelists or pastors enter into their ministries prepared to handle demonic problems. On the mission field, it is often assumed that national pastors will be able to take care of such situations, but that is not always true, especially if they have been educated in Western missionary run schools. It is true, however, that the demonstration of power in such confrontations may be a key to unlocking an apparently resistant people group."*

Upon returning to the United States in 1986, I attended a course offered by Trinity Evangelical Divinity School entitled "Power Encounter", taught by Dr. Timothy Warner. It was here that I came to realize just how much my Western worldview had prevented me from understanding the spiritual realm and its influence on the life of both believers and non-believers.

After completing this course, my wife and I were invited by Dr. Warner and his wife to be prayer partners in a personal counseling session, seeking to apply what we had learned in the classroom. Knowing that we would be ministering to an evangelical Christian seminary student, we were confident nothing weird would happen. And that was fine with us!

On our first night we sat with a young single man who recounted a 300-year history of witchcraft from his family background. He then shared how he had entered into a personal relationship with Jesus Christ through a campus ministry while in college. While there he felt called of God to enter full-time Christian service, and that was why he was attending seminary. But he was having serious problems.

We started the session with prayer, and then he shared his story. One key element was that a demonic curse had been placed on all firstborn males in his family line so that all would die before entering marriage and before the age of thirty. As he spoke he was having trouble controlling his vocal chords and could not stop clearing his throat. Kathy and I had no idea what we were about to experience.

Dr. Warner prayed and commanded all demonic spirits present to manifest themselves. His purpose was to determine if any were present and were the source of the man's difficulty in speaking.

No sooner was the prayer finished than several different, distinct and evil voices began speaking through this student. The voices claimed they had the right to be in his body and that we were powerless to help. With the kind of language they used, I now had a profound sense of why Scripture refers to them as "unclean spirits" (e.g. Matt. 10:1; Mark 1:23,26; Rev. 18:2).

As the session went on, different demonic personalities would take control of the man's vocal chords. They cursed us and continued to refuse to leave even though commanded to do so in the name of the Lord Jesus Christ. I could see in the man's eyes that he felt helpless to do anything and that he desperately wanted us to help him be free.

The session went on for hours. Sometimes the demons would answer our questions about their names and why they were harassing this believer, but they steadfastly refused to leave. In the end, we finished the session exhausted, frustrated and defeated. The feeling was as miserable as not being able to find and rescue my fellow soldiers who were captured in Nam.

The account I just shared is what would typically be called a "deliverance ministry" or a "power encounter" approach to liberating a believer from past or present demonic control. For many years Christian leaders had been recognizing that Christians were still wrestling with demonic forces in their lives post-conversion, but they had no other model with which to help these saints resolve their spiritual conflicts.

In 1988, Fuller Seminary hosted a symposium of 40 scholars who were teaching in the area of spiritual warfare at the graduate level. One of these scholars was Dr. Neil Anderson, who at the time was teaching at Talbot School of Theology in California. In the paper that he presented at the symposium, he shared his journey from the "power encounter" approach to a "truth encounter" approach. It is recorded in the book, *Wrestling With Dark Angels* (p.133):

> *"My first approach was to get a demon to expose itself and then command it to come out. Usually this resulted in a great deal of trauma for the person, and one would have to wonder who was more powerful. Although progress was made, the episode would often have to be repeated again. This is where the Epistles [New Testament letters to churches and individuals] come in. It is the believer's responsibility to resist, renounce, forgive and confess. It is not what the counselor does that results in freedom, it is what the counselee believes, confesses and renounces. The counselor acts as a facilitator. I have not attempted to 'cast out a demon' in several years, but I have seen hundreds find freedom in Christ."*

Contrary to the prevailing strategy at the time, Dr. Anderson had come to the conclusion that it is not power that sets the captive free, but truth. This resonates with Jesus' prayer for His disciples in John 17:15-17:

> *"I do not ask You to take them out of the world, but to keep them from the evil one. They are not of the world, even as*

I am not of the world. Sanctify them in the truth; Your word is truth."

After graduation from seminary in 1988, Kathy and I transitioned from our missionary work in Africa to a church planting ministry in Miami, Florida. Most of our new converts there had been involved in a syncretistic mix of old world Catholicism and African spiritism, called *Santeria*. Though we were learning, we still did not have a good understanding of how to help these new converts resolve their personal and spiritual conflicts.

In 1991 our church planting team invited Dr. Tim Warner to Miami to conduct a spiritual warfare conference. It was here that we were first introduced to the concepts found in Dr. Anderson's landmark books, **Victory Over the Darkness** and **The Bondage Breaker**.

Dr. Warner had participated in the 1988 Fuller Symposium and been profoundly impacted by what Dr. Anderson had presented there. He shared with us what he had learned. For the first time in my ministry I realized why I was having such a difficult time trying to disciple our new converts and getting them meaningfully involved in our church. The majority of these people, though born again, were still identifying themselves as victims of their past rather than victorious products of the cross of Jesus Christ. Because my attempts at discipling them were lacking the essential ingredient of grounding them in their identity in Christ, they were not growing.

Dr. Anderson described more of his journey into understanding the process of *discipleship counseling* when he wrote in his classic work, **Victory Over the Darkness** (pp16-17):

"As a pastor, I believed that Christ was the answer and truth would set people free, but I really didn't know how. People at my church had problems for which I didn't have answers, but God did. When the Lord called me to teach at Talbot School of Theology, I was searching for answers myself. Slowly I began to understand how to help people resolve their personal and spiritual conflicts through genuine repentance by submitting to God and resisting the devil.

My seminary education had taught me about the kingdom of God, but not about the kingdom of darkness... Through countless hours of intense counseling with defeated Christians, I began to understand the battle for their minds and how they could be transformed by the renewing of their minds.

I am saddened by how we have separated the ministries of discipleship and counseling in our churches. Christian discipleship too often has become an impersonal program, although good theological material is being used. Christian counseling has been intensely personal, but often lacks good theology. I believe discipleship and counseling are biblically the same. If you were a good

> *discipler you would be a good counselor and vice versa. Discipleship counseling is the process where two or more people meet together in the presence of Christ, learn how the truth of God's Word can set them free and thus are able to conform to the image of God as they walk by faith in the power of the Holy Spirit."*

A believer in Christ simply cannot run the race toward Christian maturity until he or she is free from the control of the world, flesh and the devil. What we must keep in mind is that the only Wonderful Counselor is the Lord Jesus Himself (Isaiah 9:6) and He is the One who came to set captives free (Luke 3:18). By God's grace, He will use us to rescue spiritual P.O.W.'s.

John Eldredge put it this way in his book ***Waking the Dead*** (p.150):

> *"We are at war. That war is against your heart, your Glory... Isaiah 61:1 [says]: 'He has sent me to bind up the brokenhearted, to proclaim freedom for the captives and release from darkness for the prisoners.' This is God's personal mission for his people; the offer is for us all. So, we must all be held prisoner to some form of darkness. We didn't know it – that's proof enough. In the darkness we can't see. And what is this hidden treasure [described in Isaiah 45:2,3]? Our hearts – they are the treasures hidden by*

darkness. They are not darkness; they are hidden by darkness, pinned down, held away in secret places like a hostage held for ransom. Prisoners of war."

The question that burns on our heart right now is this: Are *you* walking in the freedom that is yours in Christ or are you a spiritual P.O.W.? If you know today that you have issues in your life that are hindering you from the fullness of the Spirit, don't wait. Get help today. You can begin by praying along with us:

Dear heavenly Father, I thank You that Jesus was bound to the cross so that I could be free. He was scourged so I could be healed. He died so that I could have life. I ask You, Lord, to search me and know my heart. Test me and know my anxious thoughts, and see if there be any hurtful way in me. And please lead me in Your everlasting way. Open my eyes to any ways in which I have surrendered ground to the devil in my life so that I can close those doors and present those areas back to You. Where I need repentance, please grant it to me. Enable me to come to my senses and escape from the enemy's snares. I no longer want to live in captivity to his will, but I want to say, "Not my will, but Yours be done, O God." Please unleash all Your power, grace, truth and authority in my life so that I can experience the freedom Christ purchased for me at Calvary. In the name of the Crucified, Risen, Ascended and Glorified Lord Jesus Christ I pray, Amen.

Chapter Ten

Friendly Fire

There were many occasions during my tour in Vietnam when we brought overwhelming firepower to bear so quickly and in such close proximity to our own soldiers in combat that there was a very real danger of injuring or killing our own soldiers. This could happen at any time, but engagements after dark required extra caution on the part of those delivering this ordinance near our troops.

The hour was after midnight. We were flying another nighthawk mission over numerous ambush patrols scattered across the rice paddies and jungles. There was no moon that night, making it difficult to navigate and figure out exactly where we were as well as the lay of the land below us. To make matters worse, there were no lighted cities or highways by which we could get our bearings. It was pitch black in the air and on the ground. Pinpointing targets without shooting our own people presented a formidable challenge any night if and when we got into a firefight.

We received a radio call from one of the ground units. Their message came in whispered words so as not to be heard by the enemy soldiers approaching their position. This six-man patrol was hunkered down in fox holes near a supply trail as VC soldiers too numerous to engage in battle moved past them.

The enemy was so close to their position they could see and hear them. Normally our men would have put a strobe light in their helmet to help me locate their exact position, but this night it was not possible. Nevertheless, they were requesting our gunship support to fire on this trail just a few feet in front of them. I had a general idea of their location simply by the grid coordinates on the map strapped to my leg, but it was very risky.

One of our tactics as pilots was to fly some distance away from these ambush patrols, then drop down to an altitude just above tree top level and come back around. The VC knew we were flying above them from the sound of our rotor blades, but they couldn't see us because we never flew with our lights on. When we were out of earshot, they would think we had flown to another location and were no longer a threat. In reality, we would turn back toward them and drop to the nap of the earth so that our helicopter could not be heard until we were right on top of them.

As I drove the helicopter at maximum speed as close to the tops of the trees as I dared fly, I could see what appeared to be our unit's location. I ordered everyone to lock and load their weapons. Over the intercom I told my gunner to open fire with our mini-gun mounted out the left side of the cargo bay, just behind my seat. The firepower of this weapon was devastating, with the capacity to put a bullet into every square foot of an area the size of a football field. Its use ensured that nothing would be left standing in the target area.

As soon as my gunner pulled the trigger, the sound of which was deafening, I heard a scream in my headset from the radio operator on the ground. I will take that terrible sound to my grave. He was shouting at the top of his lungs, "Shut it off! You are shooting your own men!"

Immediately I banked the aircraft hard right and pulled up. This caused my gunner's trajectory to move up along the tree line and tear down some of the jungle foliage. We barely made it over the tops of the trees ourselves.

I thought to myself, "What have I done? Have I just killed some of our own men?"

By this time, the enemy knew we were on site, so they scattered into the jungle dragging with them the bodies of their comrades we had just killed. But I desperately wanted to know if we had just caused some needless casualties of war from our own friendly fire.

When I came back around for a second pass over the LZ, the voice on the radio assured me that our soldiers were unharmed, but that our bullets had come within inches of their foxholes. You can't imagine how relieved I felt that I had not killed some of our own men. Now that it was safer to identify their position and I could see exactly where they were located, I exhausted the remainder of our ammunition around their perimeter and kept watch over them until our fuel supply ran low.

I didn't know the names of the men below us, nor did I ever get to meet them face to face. All I knew was their call sign over a radio signal. However, that night, we were all tied together by the reality of the danger and potential damage of friendly fire.

Since our conversion to Christ in 1977, Kathy, our two daughters, Jennifer & Sarah, and I have fought shoulder to shoulder in a spiritual battle we initially understood little about. We entered into this warfare naïvely thinking that Christians, being on the same side, would never do anything to intentionally harm one another. After all, we were fellow soldiers, committed to the same vision and mission, weren't we? Why wouldn't we all agree that the most important thing in the world was to glorify God by preaching the gospel, proclaiming release to captives and setting the oppressed free together?

The Lord Jesus Himself had proclaimed that to be His mission statement (Luke 4:18-19), and the apostle John echoed that reality, writing that our Lord's purpose in coming was to destroy the devil's works (1 John 3:8). Shouldn't all God's people be on the same page as their Lord?

It is clearly God's design and desire for His children to be unified in obeying the Great Commandment and fulfilling the Great Commission. Jesus prayed for this in His high priestly prayer, recorded in John 17:14-21:

> *"I have given them Your word; and the world has hated them, because they are not of the world, even as I am not of the world. I do not ask You to take them out of the world, but to keep them from the evil one. They are not of the world, even as I am not of the world. Sanctify them in the truth; Your word is truth. As You sent*

me into the world, I also have sent them into the world. For their sakes I sanctify Myself, that they themselves also may be sanctified in truth. I do not ask on behalf of these alone, but for those also who believe in Me through their word; that they may all be one; even as You, Father, are in Me and I in You; that they also may be in Us, so that the world may believe that You sent Me."

Two thousand years ago Jesus prayed that we would be unified in love as we lived together behind enemy lines on this fallen planet. Years later, Paul exhorted believers to exhibit the unifying qualities of being of one mind, loving each other, united in spirit and intent on one purpose (Philippians 2:2).

The heart of Jesus has always been that we would manifest a deep concern and care for one another, demonstrating a unified front that would be so winsome to the unconverted, that they would see that Jesus was truly sent from God the Father. He was not talking about uniformity, but unity in diversity through the sanctifying truth of God's word. We all have different personality styles, cultural experiences and theological persuasions. Jesus was not praying that we should all look alike and act alike, only that we reflect the oneness and unity of His relationship to the Father.

The Army did not look like or operate in the same way as the Marines. The Marines were not identical to the Air Force. The Air Force was different than the Navy. But we were all on the same side, fighting side-by-side for a common cause for one another. Sadly, that has too often not been the case within the body of Christ.

According to current research, we are losing about 18,000 pastors and more than 5000 long term missionaries each year, many directly or indirectly due to friendly fire. The most common scenario involves interpersonal conflict followed by burnout and moral failure. If Christian leaders are under this kind of pressure, what makes us think those in the ranks are having it any better? If the enemy strikes the shepherds, will not the sheep be scattered?

In a monthly newsletter, Focus on the Family founder and president, James Dobson wrote in August of 1998 (p.2) said:

> *"Of great concern, of course, is the state of the clergy itself. Thousands of spiritual leaders are barely hanging on from day to day. Our surveys indicated that 80 percent of pastors and 84 percent of their spouses are discouraged or dealing with depression. More than 40 percent of pastors and 47 percent of their spouses report they are suffering from burnout, frantic schedules and unrealistic expectations. We estimate that approximately 1,500 pastors leave their assignments each month, due to moral failure, spiritual burnout or contention within their local congregations."*

World Evangelical Fellowship (WEF) conducted a survey among 553 mission agency leaders from 14 nations in 1996, seeking to uncover the reasons for the abnormal amount of missionary attrition taking place in both the "new and old world sending nations." In an address delivered to 110 representatives from over 30 nations at All Nations College in England, WEF Missions Committee Director, Dr. Bill Taylor said, "Do not be afraid to tell the new generation of missionaries the price they may be asked to pay. Illness, kidnapping and martyrdom are realities of the missionary experience today."

Reflecting on Dr. Taylor's words in the WEF newsletter dated April 9th of 1996 added this commentary:

> *"Tragic as these [above-mentioned missionary dangers] are, Bill's illustration of the returned missionary in her suicide note expressed how the lack of pastoral attention and understanding had driven her to take her life [and] brought into sharp focus the reason for the consultation. Pastoral intervention is not only needed to avert tragedies, but to help career missionaries be effective in packing heaven with worshippers! The challenge of the unreached peoples can primarily be met through long-term missionaries. We must help the right ones to get there and provide the support they need to stay there."*

Kathy and I have traveled the world. We have been confronted by the *nganga nkisi* (witch doctors) in Central

Africa, *curanderos* (psychic healers) in Central America and Mexico, *santeros* and *santeras* (priests and priestesses of the cult of Santeria) in Miami, FL and the *juju men* from West Africa. Some of them were intimidating at first, but they all understood the reality of spiritual battle. As we developed a relationship with them and they realized that we were not there to attack them, but rather show them a better way. We found most of them to be pleasant and easy people to talk with.

This has not always been true with our brothers and sisters in Christ. My entire family has been hurt by "friendly fire." It almost cost us our ministry, draining away our desire to keep moving forward. **Gossip**, theological arrogance, inflexibility, legalism, contentions over ministry philosophy, and power struggles for control are all weapons of mass destruction that have damaged us.

Sadly, I must confess that at times I too have been guilty of firing some of these devastating salvos against my own people out of frustration, pain or misunderstanding.

Don't get me wrong. I believe with all my heart that there are theological convictions that we all should have and those were clearly delineated when the apostle Paul wrote:

> *"There is one body and one Spirit, just as also you were called in one hope of your calling; one Lord, one faith, one baptism, one God and Father of all who is over all and through all and in all."*
> Ephesians 4:4-6.

Those are the things to major on, and if we do, the door is wide open for love which is the perfect bond of unity (Colossians 3:14).

However, we can easily become more committed to our theological and philosophical preferences than we are to loving each other and treating each other with kindness and compassion. This is sin and grievous to our God. <u>Over commitment to our own points of view</u> can easily become theological arrogance and cause much unnecessary collateral damage.

The Apostle Paul's heart must have been breaking when he wrote:

> *"Be angry, and yet do not sin; do not let the sun go down on your anger, and do not give the devil an opportunity... Let no unwholesome word proceed from your mouth, but only such a word as is good for edification, according to the need of the moment, so that it will give grace to those who hear. Do not grieve the Holy Spirit of God, by whom you were sealed for the day of redemption. Let all bitterness and wrath and anger and clamor and slander be put away from you, along with all malice. Be kind to one another, tender-hearted, forgiving each other, just as God in Christ also has forgiven you."* Ephesians 4:26-32.

That Scripture ought to wake up every one of us. Unresolved anger in our hearts leaves the door wide open for the devil to operate in our lives! The Greek word for "opportunity" is *topos* which means a place, in this case a base of operations by which the devil can launch a military campaign against us. In essence, harboring bitterness and unforgiveness in our hearts will give opportunity for the enemy to "tunnel underneath our lives." This does not mean that a believer in Christ can be possessed by the devil. We belong to Christ alone and have been purchased by His shed blood, (see 1 Peter 1:18-19). However, Satan can wreak havoc on any child of God who refuses to forgive, by afflicting his mind, emotions, will and even his physical body.

How dangerous to angrily hunker down into our denominational, philosophical or methodological bunkers and fire salvos at one another in the name of "being right." Yet that is what too often happens, and by so doing we foolishly leave out a welcome mat for the devil.

Tragically, our track record as Christians has been abysmal in terms of getting along. Hence the need for the apostle Paul to urge us in Ephesians 4:1-3:

> *"Therefore, I, the prisoner of the Lord, implore you to walk in a manner worthy of the calling with which you have been called, with all humility and gentleness, with patience, showing tolerance to one another in love, being diligent to preserve the unity of the Spirit in the bond of peace."*

Have you ever wondered why, in the middle of the passage on spiritual warfare in Ephesians 6, Paul felt led to remind the believers that "our struggle is not against flesh and blood [people]" but against spiritual forces (Ephesians 6:12)? It is because he just finished admonishing the saints in Ephesus and teaching them how to get along in church (Ephesians 4), in the home (Ephesians 5–6) and in the workplace (Ephesians 6).

Those primary relationships of Christian to Christian, husband to wife, wife to husband, children to parent, parent to child, employees to employer and employer to employees are the main breeding grounds for friendly fire! And Paul wanted to make sure we were shooting at the enemy, not at each other!

Have we listened? Not very well.

After more than 30 years of ministry, one of the most difficult and disheartening challenges we have had to face has been attacks from our own people. Therefore, we have come to realize that the interpersonal conflicts we experience within our own ranks are at the heart of spiritual warfare.

Satan's primary tactics are discouragement, dissension, and division. He seeks to search and destroy through a "divide and conquer" strategy. If he can find a way to drive a wedge between God's people, he can tempt us to turn our fire on one another. And the consequences and collateral damage from these internal conflicts can do devastating harm.

Although a discussion of the theology and praxis of conflict, change, confrontation and reconciliation goes well beyond the scope of this book, suffice it to say that it is one of the most critical issues in the Church today. Since interpersonal conflicts or friendly fire can strike a knockout blow to any relationship, family, church or

Christian organization, it is imperative that we grow up and learn to speak the truth in love with one another (Ephesians 4:15).

Conflict and confrontation are usually perceived as "dirty words" in Christian circles and understandably so, since few believers don't know how to play fair. However, conflict is inevitable in a fallen world, Jesus loves us anyway, even when we choose to have conflicts and become overly committed to our own points of view which equals pride. We need not fear conflict. In fact, if handled properly, it can be God's operating table for correction, healing and growth in our lives.

Confrontation, on the other hand, presents much more of a challenge to walk in the light, speak the truth in love and seek to resolve our differences before they escalate into injustices. Although forgiveness is commanded, reconciliation may not happen. Scripture says, "Be of the same mind toward one another; do not be haughty in mind, but associate with the lowly. Do not be wise in your own estimation. Never pay back evil for evil to anyone. Respect what is right in the sight of all men. If possible, so far as it depends on you, be at peace with all men" (Romans 12:16-18).

When we realize that we have hurt another brother or sister in Christ and that other person is holding something against us, we cannot worship God until we seek to make that relationship right (Matthew 5:23-24). We are instructed in that Scripture to drop what we're doing in terms of our offerings to God and go get things straightened out. Where there is humility and the yearning on both sides for truthful peace, reconciliation indeed can happen. But just as it takes two to fight, it takes two to be friends. And reconciliation cannot happen unless both sides make the choice to forgive.

The good news is that, even if the other party refuses to forgive and continues to fire his shots, we can still walk in freedom through forgiveness. Forgiveness is making the choice to cancel out the items in the debit column of relationships, no matter how many offenses are itemized there (Matthew 18:22). It is canceling the debts that others owe us by their attacks or negligence and choosing not to make them pay. It is letting them off your hook and leaving all revenge and retribution in the hands of a just, wise and merciful God (Romans 12:19).

When we make that choice to forgive, being honest with God about how we have been hurt, then He moves in with His healing hand to begin to bandage up our wounds. If we persist in our anger, resentment and unforgiveness, it will turn to bitterness and tear us up on the inside (see Matthew 18:32-35), poisoning others through our hateful words (see Hebrews 12:15).

The bottom line is that we can put a stop to our part in friendly fire by forgiving from the heart and adhering to the principles below. And by so doing, we deal a powerful blow to the enemy of our souls.

I realize that we can hurt one another unintentionally at times, but if we commit ourselves to the following relational values and rules of speech there will be far fewer casualties from friendly fire.

Relational Non-Negotiables/Values:

Love – When Jesus instructed His disciples in the upper room discourse prior to His crucifixion, He described a relationship between His followers that would be characterized by love. He taught, "A new commandment I give to you, that you love one another. By this all men will know that you are My disciples, if you have love for one another" (John 13:34-35). First Corinthians 13 describes what love looks like and will enable you to recognize when God's agape love is operating in and through your life.

Commitment – We must be committed to encouraging one another, helping each other succeed in our unique callings and speaking well of one another. Paul affirmed and exhorted the believers in Thessalonica to "encourage one another and build up one another, just as you also are doing" (1 Thess. 5:11). In a marriage relationship what will cost more, commitment or divorce?"

Loyalty – No person in a leadership role, whether he be husband, father, pastor, missionary or business leader, can survive disloyalty – especially when it comes from those closest to us. One of the enemy's greatest tactics to discourage us comes through gossip and attacks against our character and reputation. Loyalty does not mean blind allegiance or obedience. There should always be room for discussion and disagreement. Loyalty means you are faithful to the other person, desiring and seeking with all your heart to make him or her successful.

Respect – Everyone deserves our respect, no matter what their rank or position might be, because every person has been created in the image and likeness of God. Therefore, respect for who you are as a person is not something to be earned, and must be granted even to those whose behavior is not worthy of respect. Scripture says to *"Honor all people*, love the brotherhood, fear God, honor the king" (1 Peter 2:17).

These first four values of love, commitment, loyalty and respect are not optional, no matter what others have done to us. Every soldier I served with realized the need to abide by these four values whether we liked it or not.

However, in the heat of battle, where the metal meets the meat, the fifth value was absolutely essential for our very survival. It is the glue that holds armies and relationships together. It is:

Trust – We can respect people even when they have hurt us badly, though we will likely no longer trust them. Everyone deserves respect, but only those who earn it can gain our trust. Respect is a non-negotiable, but trust must be earned. If there is a breach of trust, it will take time to repair, and in some cases may never be fully restored. If there is no trust, we might work together to accomplish some common goal or objective, but there can be no lasting, meaningful relationship.

It is important to realize that God is committed to relationships in the body of Christ through loving, caring, honest, and supportive relationships. He is not and never will be satisfied with believers simply living in some kind of peaceful coexistence, declaring a cease-fire of sorts, but without any heart connection. 1 Peter 1:22 raises the bar high. It says:

"Since you have in obedience to the truth purified your souls for a sincere

love of the brethren, fervently love one another from the heart."

By the grace of God and the power of the Holy Spirit, we can do just that. And when we do, the unbelieving world will finally wake up and take notice that Jesus is for real.

Rules of Etiquette for Our Tongues (James 3:6-16):

In the Christian community we supposedly don't gossip, we just share "prayer requests." There is a very line between the two, a very fine line. Remember there is no such thing as a neutral word. Every word that leaves our lips with either bless or curse. Gossip can't kill the body, but may kill a spirit just like a bullet to the soul.

Always be quick to listen and slow to speak. Before we listen to what anyone says about us or anyone else, or what we share as "prayer requests," ask the following five questions before you listen to what others are saying or what we might share about others:

1. What is your reason for telling me this?
2. Where did you get your information?
3. Have you gone directly to the source?
4. Have you personally checked out all the facts?
5. Can I quote you if I check this out?

Always remember to engage brain and heart before opening your mouth.

Dear heavenly Father, Your word says that I can have all kinds of supernatural gifts from You and even make enormous sacrifices for Your kingdom, but if I don't have love it profits me nothing and I myself am nothing. Please forgive me for the times I have placed a higher premium on being in control or "right" and have ignored your command to love as You love. Forgive me for any hostile attitudes, slanderous words or angry actions that have damaged other brothers or sisters in Christ. Show me the ones I need to go to be reconciled with. Lord, remind me when I am hurt or frustrated or embarrassed or humiliated that my struggle is not against other people, but against the devil. I want to aim my artillery fire at him. Thank You that I can make a difference for Your kingdom by speaking the truth in love and being part of Your building crew rather than Satan's wrecking crew. By Your grace and strength alone can I do this as I pray in Jesus' name, Amen.

Chapter Eleven

The Wall

It was December 16, 1969. Another very dark night around 3:00am as we were resupplying ambush patrols in the northwestern corner of Vietnam near the Cambodian border. I had just left the LZ and was heading back to base camp to refuel and pick up more supplies for our troops in the field.

As we cleared the tree line, another of our helicopters from our unit prepared to land in this same location. They were heavy with supplies. It was a hot and humid night and none of us could see very clearly. These night time landings were always very changeling. Because of the danger of possible enemy fire in the LZ, their landing lights were not turned on until the last possible instant, making it extremely difficult to judge their approach speed and altitude.

Knowing how difficult it had been for me to execute our landing onto a piece of land about the size of a house in the middle of this tropical rain forest, I banked my aircraft to check on the other chopper coming in. I knew

The Wall

they were on short final approach to the LZ because I was talking with them over the radio. Circling back around and gaining altitude as quickly as possible, everything seemed going as planned. All of a sudden I saw the explosion below me.

No one will ever know what exactly happened in those last few seconds. All I cared about was that my friends had just crashed into the LZ. Their fuel bladders had ruptured and the explosion and fire was enormous.

Immediately, we landed within about 50 yards of their position. The heat from the crash was too intense to get any closer. As we touched down, I could see the crew desperately trying to escape the burning inferno in which they were trapped.

I ordered my crew chief to lock and load his M-16, leave our helicopter and try to rescue our friends. I kept my gunner behind his M-60 to give us covering fire if we needed it. I wanted so badly to un-strap my shoulder harness and run to their aid, but I had to remain behind the controls. I felt helpless.

To our amazement, I watched my friend, "Sugi" get out of his burning helicopter and start walking toward us. He was a human torch. His entire body was on fire. As soon as my crew chief reached him, he rolled him in the grass to put out the fire. I never expected Sugi to get back up, but he did.

The crew chief desperately tried to get to the other three crew members in the burning aircraft but they were already dead. Meanwhile, Sugi kept walking toward us. When he reached our helicopter, I could already smell his burning flesh. His flight suit and helmet had melted into his body. I couldn't believe he was still alive. He climbed into the back cargo bay and sat down. When our crew chief returned, we took off and headed south to the burn unit in Saigon 30 minutes away. There would be no adequate help for Sugi at our base camp hospital.

I never reached more than 300 feet of altitude as I pushed my cyclic stick forward to its maximum speed. We hit the landing pad in Saigon in record time and Sugi just stepped off the helicopter and walked away. I would never see him again. He died minutes later.

That day two fellow pilots and their crew died, Warrant Officer Michael Joseph Drake and Warrant Officer Leonard James Sugimoto. They had been flying that mission together. As pilots and friends, we would have done anything to help one another. I had flown missions with both these great pilots.

"Sugi" was aircraft commander the night I flew right seat with him when our engine quit over the Michelin Rubber Plantation. I am convinced that I wouldn't be writing this book had he not been with me that night when God answered the prayers of two ladies back in Illinois who were praying for us and what he did to restart our engine that night.

Nick Lappos, a fellow helicopter pilot who knew Sugi well as I did posted this note on the Vietnam Memorial Web site June 8, 2002 and wrote the following:

> *"Len Sugimoto was a fine pilot and officer. I went to flight school with Len and I remember him vividly. He was quick and athletic, and a superb pilot. His quiet sense of humor was always*

just below the surface. He married just at the end of flight school as I did, and he moved off post into temporary housing in a trailer as I remember. All of us newlyweds swapped stories of the trials of mixing flight school and a new marriage! Len volunteered to do a difficult job when his country called, and he did it the best he knew how. No country could ask more than Len gave."

In 1994, Kathy and I were very much engaged in planting a bi-lingual church in Miami, Florida. We had never visited our nation's capital and we decided it would be a good time to do so as our youngest daughter, Sarah, needed to do a field trip for a school requirement. I really didn't put much thought into the trip, nor was I thinking about what we might see there.

We arrived in Washington, DC late on a March night. It was approaching midnight and traffic was light, so we decided to drive around the White House and the Constitution Gardens to see the Washington Monument and Lincoln Memorial. Parking spaces were plentiful, so we stopped and walked into the park. Not sure you could that today in this age of the war on terrorism.

I had always wanted to see the Vietnam Veterans Memorial or "The Wall" as it is now referred to. In order to construct it, a 500-foot slice was taken out of the ground in the middle of the park. The memorial consists of two walls with the east wall pointing to the Washington Monument and the west wall pointing toward the Lincoln Memorial.

The material chosen for the memorial was black granite. The chiseled names of every soldier who died in Vietnam in that granite rock monument turns white when it rains so you can easily see the 58,267 names of those who lost their lives in Vietnam to stand out boldly. Of the 244 soldiers who were awarded the Medal of Honor during the Vietnam conflict, 153 of them are recorded on The Wall. The granite is so highly polished that it acts as an almost perfect mirror. As you stand in front of it in the sunshine, you see your image reflected back. It is a stark reminder that though the names of the dead are engraved on the wall, we on this side of life cannot reach them and they cannot reach us.

If you have never been there, it is not easy to find even in daylight. We approached from the north side and didn't see it until we were on top of it. I started down the walkway in front of the wall. I soon noticed the flowers, pictures, cards and personal items left in front of the various panels by relatives and friends that mourned the loss of a family member who died in this war.

As I reached the dividing point between the east and west walls, I stepped back onto the grassy knoll behind me, and sat down. The Wall was lit with lights. It was raining and cold. Gazing at the memorial, my emotions hit me like a runaway truck. I was overwhelmed and began to weep uncontrollably.

Both Kathy and Sarah came over and just held me. The young woman who waited until I came home from the war to marry me, and my youngest daughter born to us ten years later were now comforting their husband and father. Neither of them said a word. But they understood that a soldier had come home, and my girls were there as I wept.

The Wall

After a few moments, Kathy and Sarah left me alone to look for the names of my fallen friends inscribed on that black granite wall, like Sugi and others to help me remember my fallen comrades. They give you these pieces of paper that you can place over a name and then etch that name onto the memorial paper with a pencil.

Sarah's recollections of that night are poignant and profoundly meaningful to me. She wrote this in her journal while she was still in Junior High that night after the trip and gave it to me years later to include in this book. It was the first time I read what she wrote as I was writing this book:

"The dark shadow of The Wall swallowed my sight as I searched for my father's silhouette. The myriad of engraved names moaned with memories of the soldiers' souls. They told of terror and triumph, death and duty, suffering and salvation. Drizzles of the rendering rain dampened my pencil and paper until I reached the place on The Wall where my father found the names of his friends. Each engraved letter loaded my awareness of the missing link to this father of mine. Trembling, my dad turned to hold me, but to my astonishment it was not him. Facing me was a 19-year-old boy who had seen horrors that no human can fathom. Tears that I had never seen him shed before poured down, dropping him to his knees. So overwhelming was his grief, that I didn't

know what to do or say to comfort him. So I proceeded to trace the name of the man that burned to death before my helpless father's eyes. While each letter lifted onto the paper, the understanding dripped into my conscious mind. The reflection of the names rippled, revealing the reason for rejoicing as I realized I was not replicating my father's name. I looked in awe at this man who attempted to provide and protect what he felt was true. I understood what he had lost in order to have fought. I had seen him as a carpenter, missionary, pastor, leader, speaker, and teacher. Now I could say I knew him not only as a spiritual soldier, but as a veteran of a war that I would never understand. I am so proud to have a father and friend who has survived and surpassed the Vietnam War. That was his boot camp for the spiritual war he now fights daily. I praise the Lord who gave me my father and who promises us victory in this life and immortality in the one to come. Thank you, Dad. I had a hard time finding the right words to express myself. I am sure you had it a million times harder. I am so glad you are alive and strong, inside and out. I love you so much and am proud to be your daughter."

Your Daughter–Sarah

The Wall

Though movies can portray moments of glory in battle, war is not glorious. It is brutal, cruel, painful and bloody. Over 40 years later, I am still healing from the wounds it inflicted on my young soul. Do I regret having gone? No. It was my duty to go and I am proud that I could serve my country, fellow soldiers and the Vietnamese people I was able to serve and protect. But it's a fact of life that freedom always comes with a cost, and that cost is shed blood. I regret not doing more to gain freedom for our Vietnamese friends. Most of them treated me well other than some who were always trying to kill me.

Spiritual warfare is no different. It is not glamorous to engage the powers of darkness in seeking to rescue souls from sin and Satan. It can be very exhausting and at times dangerous work, especially as we seek to make inroads with the gospel to unreached and sometimes hostile people groups. But we should not be surprised. Our Lord Himself shed His precious blood on the cross so that we could be free from the tyranny of sin, Satan and death. Hebrews 12:3-4 exhorts us in this way:

> *"For consider Him [Christ] who has endured such hostility by sinners against Himself, so that you will not grow weary and lose heart. You have not yet resisted to the point of shedding blood in your striving against sin."*

In America right now that is true. Although some have suffered the loss of relationships, finances, jobs and reputations for their faith, we have not had to spill our blood for the sake of Christ, at least not yet. But countless others since the birth of the Christian faith have.

As one Christian said, "The most dangerous man is the one who is not afraid to die." The terrorists have learned and applied that principle for evil. Isn't it time for believers in Christ to live by that principle for good?

Chapter Twelve

Welcome Home Soldier

I returned home in September, 1970 one year to the day after I arrived in Vietnam as a new helicopter pilot entering combat in 1969. Toward the end of my tour I was promoted from Warrant Officer One, WO1 to Chief Warrant Officer Two, CW2.

Returning to the States all of us went through a military processing station in San Francisco and then on to the international airport there to get our flights home. We changed from our grubby combat flight suits and jungle fatigues into our dress uniforms after a grueling non-stop flight from Saigon.

None of us slept much on that flight from Saigon. All we cared about was that we survived our one year tours and excited to be alive and coming home to see our families and friends.

As soon as I arrived at the main terminal, I sensed something was very wrong. People were looking at me strangely in my dress uniform almost with disdain. Here I was a twenty year old kid in my officer's uniform with a chest full of medals and yet people seemed to be avoiding me. Still, I had a smile on my face and a spring in my step. I was going home. I had survived the war.

I needed to fly to Chicago's O'Hare airport to meet my family where I grew up, so I hurried to the ticket counter to make connections. As I approached the line at the counter, I greeted those around me and told them how happy I was to be back safe and secure. I couldn't wait to get on the flight to Chicago.

As I waited my turn in line I could hear people mumbling derogatory remarks about our involvement in the Vietnam War. I turned around to ask them about their concerns. A young man and his wife looked me right in the eyes and called me a "f — — — baby killer."

I was stunned and didn't know how to respond. I never killed any babies. I did kill lots of VC (Viet Cong Guerilla Soldiers) and NVA (North Vietnamese Army Regulars), but I never killed any babies. At that moment every ounce of joy, energy and courage left in my soul drained out of me. I thought to myself, "Wasn't it for you that I went to fight?"

For the record, I used to fly over the village of Cu Chi many nights outside of our perimeter to protect our friends who came onto our base camp that had over 20,000 soldiers and one of the largest airstrips outside of Saigon every day to do our cooking, cleaning, and many other service projects. They were good people and I enjoyed interacting with them even if we didn't always understand one another well because of the language barriers.

The name of the wife and mother who took care of the 10 pilots I was living with in our hootch every day was Bai. She was only 35 and already had eight children of her own. I would always give her my C-Rations and whatever local currency I had in my pocket. She was a wonderful lady with always a smile on her face.

Many nights when I turned on the spot light from my helicopter just 50 feet over their thatched roofed homes I could see the faces of the VC holding them hostage as they fired mortars and rockets into our base camp. I knew where Bai lived and wanted to kill anyone trying to hurt her or her family. I couldn't fire back without killing our Vietnamese friends and their families. I felt helpless and hopeless whenever this happened. You don't want to know how they abused these families. The VC were the baby killers, not us.

Also, I was one of only a few pilots who would volunteer to fly supply missions for the Catholic Nuns operating the leper colonies in our area. It was never dangerous because the VC and NVA wouldn't dare go near them as their animistic worldview thought these places to be inhabited by demons. I had a fun time after landing and unloading supplies with the Sisters and the lepers. Their faces will be forever etched on my heart.

As a twenty year old veteran of the Vietnam Conflict perhaps I was naïve in thinking that the greatest love a man could show for his country or others was his willingness to lay down his life for the downtrodden, whether they spoke English or Vietnamese.

In the San Francisco airport after my encounter with this critical young couple, if I would have had civilian clothes in my bag I would have changed into them immediately before getting on my flight to Chicago. I felt rejected and ashamed. What damage a critical spirit can inflict ☹

When I arrived in Chicago, my whole family was there to greet me. I was so tired and disillusioned that I could barely enjoy their welcome. It was as if I were in some kind of time warp. I could hardly hear what they were saying to me, and their words only ricocheted off my heart. Nevertheless, it was so nice to see my wonderful parents and ten younger brothers and sisters all of whom are still alive as I write these words. This chapter is dedicated to them.

Arriving at my house, I got out of my uniform right away and took a hot bath for the first time in years. I put on some of my old clothes because I yearned to settle back into familiar surroundings and pretend that I had never left home. I was skin and bones and suffering physically from my tour of duty in Southeast Asia. My mom, who is a nurse, fretted over me my first night home because she didn't know what I needed. But she did a great job of fattening me up and getting me healthy again.

That night I laid down in my old bed and slept soundly well into the next day. I was exhausted physically, mentally, emotionally and totally empty spiritually. A son and a brother who had left as a starry-eyed 18 year-old boy and went to war was home again. But I was not the same man. I was tired, confused, bitter and broken.

After World War II, veterans had the time and opportunity to process what they had gone through over their years of combat in that global conflict. It was a war in which the lines between good and evil were more clearly drawn. Most of them returned on ships that could take a month or more to reach our shores. But with the Vietnam conflict, one night you could be flying a helicopter gunship mission over the steamy Mekong Delta and within

48 hours be back on the streets of your home town. The transitional shock was enormous to say the least.

I remember dropping in on some friends after returning home, trying to reconnect with them. They'd ask me, "Where have you been? We haven't seen you for a while." They spoke as if I'd been gone only a few weeks. I would usually respond, "I was in Nam for the last year." As soon as I started to talk about what it was like, they would change the subject. They didn't want to hear about it. My family, friends and even my country were not able to help me make the transition from soldier to civilian.

I was flying combat missions in Vietnam on May 4, 1970 when our own National Guard soldiers were called to Kent State University in Ohio to quell the anti-war demonstrations being held on that campus. When it was all over, four young students lay dead and ten others were wounded. That was a tragic moment in our nation's history for all Americans, no matter what side of the controversial war they were on.

It is one of our most precious freedoms that gave people the right to protest the war in Vietnam and still gives us the right to protest any other war for that matter. What concerns me is that during and after Vietnam, the American people abused that freedom. Going beyond their right to protest the war effort, many of them leveled their attacks against the warriors sent into that war. And that was terribly wrong.

Twenty-one years after returning from Vietnam, Kathy and I were church planting among the Cuban population in Miami, Florida. We had established several bi-lingual cell groups in our neighborhood in western

Dade County. We were some of the few "gringos" living in this fast growing area.

We were preparing to launch our first Sunday morning services in the ballroom on the campus of Florida International University near our home. The county fair is held on this campus each year and we went on Saturday.

It was your typical county fair. There were carnival rides, 4-H displays, hawkers at their booths selling anything and everything, and displays from a variety of local, county and state governmental organizations. The air was filled with noise, laughter and shouting in several different languages. It was sort of an organized chaos of good times, good smells and good music.

Kathy and I strolled comfortably through the displays sampling the different ethnic foods and purchasing all the unnecessary stuff that later ends up in garage sales. Kathy walked on ahead of me as something caught my eye. I noticed a canvas wall full of pictures and several tables set up with military paraphernalia from the Vietnam War.

I stopped to examine the memorabilia from an era in my life that I thought was long since over. As I stood there, I was captured by the items on the table as they took me back to the sights and sounds of war. Looking up, I noticed a man and woman standing behind the display booth watching me. They must have observed my interest in their display.

While I was engrossed in the objects on display, absorbed in memories of the Vietnam war, the couple walked up to the table, stood in front of me and said hello. Having caught my attention, they looked me in the eye and said together, **"Welcome home, soldier."** Somehow they just knew.

It was as if they had pulled out a .45 caliber hand gun and shot me in the chest. I dropped to my knees and began to weep uncontrollably. I had never heard anyone say that to me even though I had risked everything in Vietnam. I didn't know that there were so many bottled-up emotions inside of me, but they knew. I had learned to "stuff it" and compartmentalize my memories of combat.

Their words broke an emotional dam that I had built over the years to protect myself from all of war's painful experiences I never dealt with. Pain that I had never shared with anyone, not even Kathy came spilling out.

I now found myself on the saw dust floor in front of their display booth crying like a baby. People walking by thought I was crazy, but I didn't care. Tears of healing were freely flowing down my face. I looked up to see Kathy turning around to see where I had gone. She immediately came running to my side, not understanding what had just happened. I think she thought that someone had hurt me.

Through my sobs I told her what had just happened. She lifted me to my feet and held me. It was one of the sweetest moments and hugs, something I'll remember forever. She didn't say anything. She didn't have to. I knew that she understood. She had lived with me through so many years of the nightmares and fallout in my life as a young soldier.

She thanked the couple and led me down the sawdust path of the fairgrounds, out into the fresh air. We sat on a bench together and she held me and let me cry.

In June of 1991 our troops returned home from the first Gulf War in Iraq. They were met with a ticker tape, victory parade in our nation's capital. I remember turning on the news channel and watching them ride down our city streets celebrating and being cheered on by the majority of Americans and the news media. It was an emotional catharsis for most of us, especially Vietnam veterans. It was a magical moment for me personally, helping lift me out of my post-Vietnam trauma, for our nation did not say "thank you" or give us this kind of recognition. I relished and identified with the enthusiasm and joy of our troops that day as we welcomed them home. It was as if I were riding in the parade with them.

Today I am board member of the East Tennessee Military Affairs Council. Through our non-profit ministry, Living Legacy International, we have sent thousands of pounds of Christmas care packages to our troops overseas, especially Iraq and Afghanistan.

Child of God, you may never be thanked, honored or applauded on planet earth for your service to the King in this spiritual war. Instead you may even be called all kind of names and be treated with cruelty and contempt. But take courage! One day Jesus will personally see to it that you are safe in His arms, because you'll be home. In Revelation 7:9-17 John records the vision of such a moment:

> *"After these things I looked, and behold, a great multitude which no one could count, from every nation and all tribes and peoples and tongues, standing before the throne and before the Lamb, clothed in white robes, and palm branches were in their hands; and they cry out with a loud voice,*

saying, "Salvation to our God who sits on the throne, and to the Lamb." And all the angels were standing around the throne and around the elders and the four living creatures; and they fell on their faces before the throne and worshiped God, saying, Amen, blessing and glory and wisdom and thanksgiving and honor and power and might, be to our God forever and ever. Amen.

Then one of the elders answered, saying to me, these who are clothed in the white robes, who are they, and where have they come from? I said to him, My lord, you know. And he said to me, these are the ones who come out of the great tribulation, and they have washed their robes and made them white in the blood of the Lamb. For this reason, they are before the throne of God; and they serve Him day and night in His temple; and He who sits on the throne will spread His tabernacle over them. They will hunger no longer, nor thirst anymore; nor will the sun beat down on them, nor any heat; for the Lamb in the center of the throne will be their shepherd, and will guide them to springs of the water of life; and God will wipe every tear from their eyes."

And again, in Revelation 21:3-7:

"And I heard a loud voice from the throne, saying, Behold, the tabernacle of God is among men, and He will dwell among them, and they shall be His people, and God Himself will be among them, and He will wipe away every tear from their eyes; and there will no longer be any death; there will no longer be any mourning, or crying, or pain; the first things have passed away. And He who sits on the throne said, Behold, I am making all things new. And He said, Write, for these words are faithful and true. Then He said to me, it is done. I am the Alpha and the Omega, the beginning and the end. I will give to the one who thirsts from the spring of the water of life without cost. He who overcomes will inherit these things, and I will be his God and he will be My son."

None of us knows the day or the hour that Christ will split the skies and return like the lightning flashing from the east to the west. (Matt. 24:27). Then it will all be over. There will be no more spiritual battles. No more opportunities for heroism in the kingdom of God. The judgment will come. Time will be no more. And rewards will be granted by the King to His servants.

There will be the *crown of life* for those who have been approved by the Lord as having persevered under trials (James 1:12). There will be the *imperishable wreath* to those who in exercising self-control have run the race and fought the fight to win (1 Corinthians 9:24-27). There will be the *crown of exultation* for those who have invested their lives in others for the kingdom of God (1 Thessalonians 2:19,20). There will be the *crown of righteousness* that the Lord Jesus will award one day to all who have loved His appearing (2 Timothy 4:8). And there will be the *crown of glory* for faithful shepherds who have served under the Chief Shepherd (1 Peter 5:2-4).

Though the judgment for our sins has fully fallen on Christ, so that all who trust in Him alone to save them are forever forgiven, there remains yet a judgment for our works. For that warrior, the apostle Paul, wrote in 1 Corinthians 3:10-15:

> *"According to the grace of God which was given to me, like a wise master builder I laid a foundation, and another is building on it. But each man must be careful how he builds on it. For no man can lay a foundation other than the one which is laid, which is Jesus Christ. Now if any man builds on the foundation with gold, silver, precious stones, wood, hay, straw, each man's work will become evident; for the day will show it because it is to be revealed with fire, and the fire itself will test the quality of each man's work. If any man's work which he has built on it remains, he will receive a reward. If any man's work is burned up,*

> *he will suffer loss; but he himself will be saved, yet so as through fire."*

It's not too late. Even if you have not run the race well or fought the good fight so far, you can start over today. Don't wait. ***Today*** if you hear God speaking to you, it is time to enlist as a good soldier of Christ Jesus. "Suffer hardship with me, as a good soldier of Christ Jesus. No soldier in active service entangles himself in the affairs of everyday life, so that he may please the one who enlisted him as a soldier" (2 Timothy 2:3,4).

There is no earthly pleasure or treasure that is worth forfeiting the glory of seeing the Lord Jesus face to face, having Him wrap His arms around you, wiping away every tear and hearing Him say, "Welcome home, soldier. Well done, good and faithful servant. Enter into the joy of your Master" (see Matt. 25:14-30).

The following prayer and others in this book at the end of some the chapters come from our good friend, Rich Miller, President of Freedom in Christ Ministries:

> *Dear heavenly Father, it is much too easy to live in the light of today or even tomorrow yet forget about eternity. I confess that too often I have allowed myself to become entangled in the affairs of everyday life – living as a civilian when I'm called to be a soldier. This day, however, I hear Your voice, Your call, to lay up treasures in heaven rather than accumulating stuff on earth. I hear You urging me to see others in my home, my*

workplace, my church and my community in light of eternity. I need You to open my eyes to see things as You see them, and to live in light of the judgment of works that is to come. I long to see my life as a huge treasure of gold, silver and precious stones, not as a worthless pile of wood, hay and straw. Empower me by Your Holy Spirit to live for Your glory and to run the race, finish the course and fight the good fight of faith in this world until You call me home. In Jesus' name, Amen.

Chapter 13

A Wife's Perspective of War & Marriage

Life is a journey down an unmarked path. None of us knows where it will take us with its many twists and turns. I was only thirteen years old and Joe was fourteen when we first met. I was a young, starry-eyed romantic who thought our relationship would always be lined with flowering trees and sunshine.

Many years ago I watched as the man God had chosen to be my partner for life became a raw recruit in boot camp. And the 12 months that he would spend at war would end up haunting Joe and me for years.

The journey I stepped into the day I married Joe in 1970 was not one of flowering trees and sunshine. Instead, dark storm clouds rolled in, obscuring the sun. Littered in our path were the bewildering, painful memories and fallout from a place in Southeast Asia, an area of the world unknown to me called Vietnam.

There are some things we never forget. They may pass out of the front part of our memory, but they are always somewhere in the back of our minds swirling around and the least little thing forces us to recall and face them. Traumatic and hurtful experiences of life have a way of controlling and manipulating us, causing us to form false identities.

Insidiously, Joe's painful, embedded memories of war became a mutual part of our life together. The anguishing experiences from Vietnam that were securely locked in Joe's subconscious surfaced nightly in the form of relentless, tormenting nightmares. He tried desperately to be free, but he was imprisoned by what he had seen and had to do. He was a prisoner of war, being held captive by a mind filled with dark and unforgettable events.

What he spoke out during those nightmares went beyond my comprehension. Night after night I tried to comfort him, but nothing I did would stop or even ease his troubled soul.

More than four decades have passed since those nights of terror began. Looking back from the perspective of God's word, it is clear now that the horrific memories from the Vietnam War were certainly one of Satan's tools designed to weaken and cripple my husband.

At that point in our lives, however, I did not understand that we were in a spiritual battle. What I did know was that my sympathy and love for Joe was not sufficient. I couldn't fix him. I only wanted to be his wife. He needed something more and someone greater than me to heal his damaged emotions. It was tearing at our lives and destroying our relationship with one another. Nevertheless, we desperately wanted our marriage to work and we both wanted it badly enough to do whatever was necessary to make it healthy.

It is clear now that one of the reasons (no doubt the main reason) we survived and grew deeper in love with each other was our encounter with the Lord Jesus Christ. The Apostle Paul's words in Romans 5:6-8 still echo in my ears as I recall that bright October day in 1977 when our cry for help was answered.

Our search had led us to a pastor named Rev. Willis Reed, a retired army chaplain from World War II, who is now at home with the Lord. He listened to our story of helplessness and with an understanding that only comes from the Spirit of God, he lovingly read this passage to us from the Bible Romans 5:7-8:

> *"For while we were still helpless, at the right time Christ died for the ungodly. For one will hardly die for a righteous man; though perhaps for the good man someone would dare to die. But God demonstrates His own love toward us, in that while we were yet sinners, Christ died for us."*

The truth of the word of God penetrated my hungry heart, and two weeks later I came to a personal relationship with Jesus Christ. Joe, too, cried out in his brokenness and received Christ that very same day. Our journey then took a miraculous turn, one that has brought us into full-time ministry and the writing of this book.

You have read about some of the memories that Joe tried so hard to forget. However, God in His divine love, wisdom and tender mercy has shown us both that

trying to remember has worked much better than trying to forget.

The lessons I learned in the early years of our journey are still with me today. One of those is that being set free from our past may happen quickly or it may be a step by step process. For Joe, freedom and healing from the tormenting memories of Vietnam did not come immediately. In fact, the memories are still with him today, though the torment and fear is being replaced with freedom and faith. His memories of that time and place, some still as vivid today as the day they occurred, have been used by God that he is now courageously sharing this message of freedom in Christ with other "prisoners of war."

We have also learned that it is what we allow God to do with our experiences that makes all the difference. You know that you are healed when painful and hurtful events and experiences from your past no longer control your present nor dictate who you are as a person.

As I watched my husband continue to suffer many nights, even after our conversion to biblical Christianity, I would cry out to the Lord in prayer. It was during those dark hours that I learned to fight for him when he was too weak to do battle on his own. It helps to remember that we are not only wives, but fellow-soldiers in this freedom fight. Learning how to stand beside our husbands with the weapon of prayer is powerful in defeating the enemy's attempts to steal, kill and destroy. Prayer truly is a "weapon of mass reconstruction" (2 Cor. 10:3-5).

Somehow I feel I am not alone. I know that there are countless brothers and sisters in Christ who have been awakened to the reality of spiritual warfare. You are probably among them, or you wouldn't have picked up this book in the first place. Like me, you are learning how to use the weapons of warfare for the welfare of those you love, to the glory of God.

Be encouraged! For Joe and I, the journey that began on a path littered with painful memories that could have destroyed us is now more than 40 years old. It is a testimony of God's faithfulness to answered prayer and His eagerness to set us and other captives free.

As a woman, wife and mother, I encourage you, NO, I challenge you to step boldly into this cosmic battle for our men. As our Cuban friends in Miami would often say to us during our church planting ministry there, ***"Estamos juntos aqui en la lucha."*** Roughly translated this means, "We are here in the battle together."

Wedding - October 3rd, 1970
It was only yesterday

Celebrating our 42nd wedding anniversary - October, 2012

Epilogue

Many said that the United States should have never deployed troops to Vietnam. After all it was never declared a war, just a "conflict." The rules of engagement and our purposes there became blurred and the military strategies and the missions we flew never seemed to accomplish any significant long lasting results. Those of us who grew up in the sixties didn't have many choices. It was either the draft which required two years of service or to enlist for three years. If you enlisted there we some options for what you were going to do in Vietnam other than, like most, became ground pounders or grunts trudging through the rice paddies and mountainous jungles always trying to avoid booby traps, ambushes and many times fighting overwhelming odds with the enemy.

Toward the end of my tour it was very frustrating at times to have to call for permission to fire back when fired upon. The war just didn't make sense any longer. Morale among our troops deteriorated rapidly and we all just hoped to make it through our one year tours and come home alive. For Kathy and me it has been almost five decades of life, love, marriage and family. We are now in the second half of our lives. When we first met in 1964 in High School we had no idea that we would have ever been on such a dangerous and yet fulfilling quest. But then God! He powerfully stepped into our lives seven years after we were married and turned our lives right side up. It has been a spell binding, global journey ever since. We are yet to get our arms around everything we have experienced together.

As of this writing there have been some new challenges we could never have predicted nor desired.

We have shared Kathy's battle with cancer and my struggles with PTSD to deal with a very unpopular war in Vietnam. When we married in 1970 at the age of twenty, we had no idea that we would be where we are today.

Kathy has been through hell and back battling a very rare form of blood cancer over the last four years, Mantle Cell Lymphoma. We did everything we knew at the time when she was first diagnosed. The intense chemo therapy and an autologous stem cell transplant from her own stem cells she endured for one year put her into remission for three years. When she relapsed in 2012 the options were not what we felt we needed or wanted to do again.

So, our oldest daughter, Jennifer, the "bulldog" researcher of our family, arranged an interview with a leading hematologist at Cornell Weil University in New York. He spent three hours with us in his office and then referred us to his colleague at the Sarah Cannon Cancer Research Center in Nashville, TN to get Kathy into a new clinical trial. She is taking two pills a day of a new B-Cell Inhibitor that is keeping her in a significant level of remission. After one year she is doing well without more chemo therapy nor having to do a donor transplant.

Epilogue

We don't know where this life of ours will lead us. However, we do know that we are more than just survivors. With God's help we are thrivors. Nevertheless, we are planning to stir up more good trouble over the next twenty years. Then, we will be more than prepared and would love to see Jesus face-to-face. That will be a grand day with no more tears, suffering, wars, disease or conflicts of any kind. We can't wait to sit in His lap and hear Him say, "Welcome home My good and faithful servants." That will be a glorious day indeed ☺

To put this book into perspective we will leave you with a quote from one of our favorite authors, John Eldridge, from his book *Waking the Dead* (pp.12-13) as he reminds us that:

> *"We are at war...I don't like that fact any more than you do, but the sooner we come to terms with it, the better hope we have of making it through to the life we do want. This is not Eden. You probably figured that out. This not Mayberry, this is not Seinfeld's world, this is not Survivor. The world in which we live is a combat zone, a violent clash of kingdoms, a bitter struggle unto death. I am sorry if I'm the one to break this news to you: you were born into a world at war, and you will live all your days in the midst of a great battle, involving all the forces of heaven and hell and played out here on earth."*

To order additional copies of

Be Strong & Courageous

Please send $25 for shipping and handling to:

**Living Legacy International
P.O. Box 51903
Knoxville, TN 37950-1903**